ORGANIZING

—— FOR ——

SUCCESS

ORGANIZING

— FOR —

SUCCESS

Second Edition

KENNETH ZEIGLER

New York   Chicago   San Francisco   Lisbon   London
Madrid   Mexico City   Milan   New Delhi   San Juan
Seoul   Singapore   Sydney   Toronto

The **McGraw·Hill** Companies

4 5 6 7 8 9 0   QFR / QFR   1 5 4 3

ISBN 978-0-07-173956-6
MHID   0-07-173956-4

McGraw-Hill books are available at special quantity discounts to use as premiums
and sales promotions, or for use in corporate training programs. To contact a repre-
sentative, please e-mail us at bulksales@mcgraw-hill.com.

This book is printed on acid-free paper.

This book is dedicated to my best friend and mentor, my father, whose love, understanding, advice, and the way he lives everyday, inspires me to not give up and always strive for excellence.

—KZ

Contents

ORGANIZING

— FOR —

SUCCESS

INTRODUCTION

The 4th Dimension of Time Management—How to Increase Your Productivity and Work More Effectively with Others

Are you tired of reading the same old ideas, only they have been paraphrased and changed slightly so they seem new? Even though this topic has changed radically over the past four to five years, many writers are still putting a spin on old ideas rather than looking for new ideas and strategies to more effectively handle a significantly greater workload the average person faces every day.

Back in 1996, the Hertz car rental company began to ask why they were getting so many complaints from their managers that they were stressed out. They noticed an increase in manager turnover and employee dissatisfaction, but they couldn't understand it since every manager at Hertz had a Franklin Day Planner. After all, back in those days you weren't anyone unless you had a Franklin Day Planner. In fact, the bigger the Day Planner, the more organized you must be, people deduced.

I offered to observe their managers in the field and tell them what the problem was and propose some potential solutions. After

1

six months, I made my report to Hertz and made my recommendations. Here is that summation:

1. The Franklin Day Planner was the wrong planning tool for their field managers. Since they were rarely at their desk, the Day Planner was too large and cumbersome for them to take with them wherever they went. As a result they hardly used it.

2. I recommended that they use a very small spiral note pad or a single sheet of paper they could put in their back pocket that was more portable and thus more useful. The key is they needed a very portable tool or it wouldn't be very useful. When they returned to their desk *eventually* they could then transfer their notes and to-dos on to their calendar.

3. Hertz managers couldn't even remember what they had done two days before, when I asked them. This is because they rarely wrote anything down and did everything the second it was requested.

4. Their daily plan was unrealistic because they tried to make a "typical" day fit their plan. I recommended that they clearly understand what a "typical" day really looked like and develop a plan that took "advantage" of what a "typical" day was really like.

5. Since their plan wasn't realistic it rarely worked, so they had to work longer hours just to get the work that had to be done daily, done by the "end of the day."

6. Delegation was the number one problem I observed. Since managers didn't really understand why and how to effectively

delegate it rarely worked, so they broke down the confidence of the person they delegated to and they ended up having to still do the task, project, or report. They lost any chance to leverage their time and abilities.

7. Since they did almost everything themselves they ended up working more hours. They also had very little mental separation between work and home, so even when they weren't at work they still thought about work all the time. Thus it was like they never left work when they came in the following day. This added to the burnout. That is why I recommend putting mental closure on every day.

Even though Corporate America has significantly downsized and we are doing the work that three to four individuals used to do, we are still using the same skills set we had years ago when the workload was much less. Because of this phenomenon we are actually becoming less efficient and the result is longer hours at work each day. The number three reason for procrastination is being *overwhelmed*. As a person becomes more overwhelmed they actually slow down.

From years of research, one thing is certain, productivity has actually been decreasing over the past four to five years (even though the government's measurement of productivity is telling us that the American worker has actually never been more productive.) Is it that they are actually more productive or that they are working more hours at the same pay? I propose the later is true.

The purpose of this book is to question, "Why are you doing, what you're doing, when you're doing it?" With clear thought, do you have a reason for choosing each task or activity that you pick all day long or are you a creature of habit? Are you just trying to keep your head above water or do you have a logical reason for every activity you choose to work on throughout the day? The faster you go throughout the day, the less logical reasoning you will use and the less control you will experience.

My definition of time management is that there is a time and a place for everything. Is your reasoning or thought process that logical? This book will show you how to develop this logical thought process which in turn will actually help you focus on and accomplish more of what matters most each day.

THE HISTORY OF THIS BOOK

Since I don't believe the problem is the time system people use (e.g., Outlook, Lotus Notes, or a paper calendar), this book will focus on giving you tips, tools, ideas, and strategies that you can apply to see immediate, measurable improvement, both at work and at home. You will notice that I'm not trying to sell you an expensive day planner or any kind of electronic gadget.

There are plenty of those already, and they can be useful tools. Instead, this book can help you use whatever system you currently use more effectively. I do recommend an electronic instead of paper calendar because of the need to coordinate work and schedules.

Since traditional to-do lists (whether paper or the task function electronically) and day planners haven't really worked in a long time I recommend using a Master List. Back in 1996 I was the first to recommend a different approach other than Franklin's system. Now today, this concept is becoming increasing popular as more and more authors now recommend the same approach.

Since people have very little control over a "typical" chaotic day, traditional prioritization and structured systems don't work well. As a result there has been a dramatic increase in the number of classroom participants who come to work and "wing-it" (meaning they don't have plan at all). This is why I will show you a more flexible way to organize that can change as your day or week does.

Finally, there is very little new material on productivity. Most of it is a rehash of old, tired ideas that don't apply in this new day and age. The problem is that people are doing the work of three to four workers, yet they are approaching each day with the same mindset and organizational approach as they did when the work was less and the pace much slower.

I will offer you a new approach that will

1. Cut down on the number of hours you spend at work
2. Improve the quality of your work
3. Improve the number of tasks/projects/activities you complete every day
4. Reduce the number of times you have to do something before you achieve your desired objective
5. Increase the quality of your personal life
6. Reduce your stress
7. Put you back in control of your day and week

The key is to building a more productive day/week is to be willing to examine everything, that is, each event or activity that impacts your day and ask, "Was this the best use of my time, at this moment?" Would this activity have taken less time to complete if it was moved to a different day and/or time slot? Change is typically very uncomfortable. Are you desperate enough, discouraged enough, or stressed out enough to look for new ways to approach your day and week that will make you more productive and your life easier and more rewarding?

The key to getting organized for success is to determine and analyze when you're working on certain activities and your reasoning for these actions. In other words, use clear thought, step back from the trenches of everyday life, and analyze your activities.

This book will have you analyze:

- Why you're doing it
- What you're doing
- When you're doing it

THE BEST WAY TO START

I recommend that you read the book from the beginning. The first chapter is new to the book. I recommend that you keep track of your time for a week before you read the rest of this book. In the book you will find the Website address which contains the "Timekeeping Journal" expressly for this purpose. I'm constantly amazed that this is one of the few courses to recommend this.

Back in 1996, I began recommending the Timekeeping Journal because when I asked Hertz employees what they had done two days before, more than 90 percent couldn't specifically recall. Don't you need to know where you're starting from in order to know where you want to go?

Download the Time Journal and print it out. To get the most benefit from these lessons, begin by keeping a journal of how you spend your time for one week. I recommend keeping track of your work and personal life. It comes with instructions. Basically, you fill out the left side of each page, at the end of your day, with what you plan to do tomorrow when you return. Now go home.

Be sure that you keep track of both your work and personal time. You may wonder, "Why keep track of my personal time?" I believe a personal life is all about quality, not necessarily about quantity. Does what you're doing after work reinforce your personal mission statement? Sometimes a closer look may raise questions and lead to change.

When you return to work the next day, begin writing down what actually happens in each time block on the right side of the page. Now you really know what a "typical" day is like and you are ready to begin reading this book. Put your Time Journal to the side for the time being. Later, you will take it out again and I will show you how to find up to two more hours a day. You may be surprised how much time you find!

Every principle, suggestion, and tip in this book will take on more meaning and immediacy if you have completed the Timekeeping Journal in advance of studying this book—I feel so strongly about this that it is a requirement for each student who takes my course in person.

WHY TYPICAL APPROACHES DON'T WORK

I'm shocked at how many time management courses talk about the ability to change time and reality. Instead, I say, "Embrace reality and see what you can do to take advantage of it." This book was written with a "typical" chaotic day in mind, not some day that doesn't really exist.

When you keep track of your time for a week, you will see patterns in activities, tasks, interruptions, and unplanned events. Once you see those patterns, use the strategies discussed in this book to handle them more effectively. A major question should be, "How do I want to organize my day now that I can see reality?" You'll be amazed at the results!

In addition, you must realize that there are two aspects to saving time and becoming more productive:

1. Improving your time management skills
2. Training others so their time management skills don't kill you

This is another concept that you will probably not see or hear elsewhere. Others try to make you believe that if only your skills were better, everything would be fine. That would be great, but that's not the truth. Time management is also a "team" subject. That is why the 4th dimension of time management is a team concept. We spend most of our days "killing each other" with:

- Interruptions
- Poorly written, vague e-mails without a cooperative tone
- Immediate requests that aren't really needed immediately
- Poor response time to each other's requests
- Poorly organized communication, requests, and answers that need to be clarified

- Shallow relationship building that is closer to procrastination than really building stronger working relationships

If we could have some ground rules for engagement and working more effectively with each other, we could get much more done each day.

You will see that many of the tips, ideas, and suggestions are directed toward training others to be more efficient when dealing with you. Remember, if you don't respect your time, who will?

HOW TO USE THIS BOOK

This book is for all people who would like to become more efficient, get more done in less time, and have balance in their life. This book is written as a self-study. All the answers are contained in this book. The answers are often different for each person. Take the ones you like, make positive changes, and discard the rest. Use the Time Management Action Plan in the back of the book to write down the tips, ideas, or strategies that you're going to implement immediately after you complete this book. This activity will strengthen and reinforce your commitment to changing and improving your life, both at work and at home.

LIGHTS, CAMERA, ACTION!

The key is action. There are more than 300 tips, ideas, and strategies. Pick the ideas and strategies that apply to you, take action, and make them work. Take two or three ideas or strategies at a time and work on them until they become habits. Then move on to two or three more. Don't try to completely re-tool yourself immediately. Most of the time, you just need to tweak your current skills, habits, and way you work each day.

It can be easy to get discouraged; there is no perfection. For example, I have this conversation all the time a few weeks after a class. The student asks me, "What did you do to me?" To which I respond, "What do you mean?" The student then explains, "Well, after the class I tried what you said and it worked. Then the next day I went back to the old me, then the new me. Now I don't know who's going to show up tomorrow!" Remember, it can take up to 30 days to reset a habit, so be patient. It will get better if you keep trying. As you will see, the Ringmaster is very patient and willing to take a long-term perspective.

Any authors or trainers who tell you that their suggestions will work all the time are foolish. But consider this: If this book could make three out of five days better (that's 60 percent), wouldn't you be happy? I am!

1

Lost, But Making Excellent Time: The Key Is to Figure Out What You Want to Improve by Figuring Out What's Going Wrong

The airline pilot announced over the intercom, "I've got good news and bad news. The good news is that we're making excellent time. The bad news is I have no idea where we are. I think we're lost!

—FROM *LOST BUT MAKING EXCELLENT TIME*, BY DR. JODY SEYMOUR

THE REASONING FOR KEEPING TRACK OF YOUR TIME

How do you know where you want to get to unless you know where you are starting from? My definition of stress is, "Stress is the uncomfortable difference between the ways things are and the way you'd like them to be." You will develop a far more effective action plan if you accurately know where and on what you are spending your time on each day. Sometimes we confuse activity with productivity. As you will see, they can often be quite different. How many times have you gotten to the end of the day, felt exhausted, but when you looked at your to-do list realized everything you meant to accomplish that day was still on your list? Have you ever wondered, "Why can't I ever seem to get my own work done?"

We are moving so fast all day long, oftentimes just trying to make it until the end of the day. Maybe if I slowed down and stepped back, I could see what was really happening and look for some possible solutions. Think of it like you have a whiteboard in front of you. First, write down everything you need to get done; throw in interruptions, then unplanned events. If you could see it all clearly, how would you organize it more effectively so you could fit it all into, say, a nine hour day? The Timekeeping Journal and this book will help you do that.

Most people know they are being interrupted frequently, but they don't accurately know how often and by whom. When I ask people who have kept the Timekeeping Journal what the biggest realization they had when they reflected on what they saw in the journal after they finished, the majority said they had no idea they had as many interruptions as they saw in their Timekeeping Journals.

In many instances they noticed that 80 percent of their interruptions were coming from 20 percent of the people they interacted with. It was a far better defined group than they imagined. They could also see a pattern in the form the interruptions were taking (e.g., e-mail, phone, and face-to-face).

The strategies, ideas, and tips you will read in this book will definitely make more sense if you keep track of your time for a week before you continue to read this book. I know you may be overwhelmed and feel a little desperate but if such feelings have gone on this long, what's another week?

LET'S GET STARTED BY DOWNLOADING THE TIMEKEEPING JOURNAL

If you agree with my assessment and want to save up to two hours or more a day, go to http://www.kztraining.com/timekeepingjournal/

Download the Timekeeping Journal. There is no charge. There are enough sheets for you to keep track of five days. Print out the journal and put it on a clipboard. I recommend keeping track of all five days so you can see different patterns on different days. Also, five days is a better measurement of productivity than a single day. On the whole, five days of keeping track of your time should provide you with a very accurate picture for you to work with.

HOW TO KEEP THE JOURNAL FOR BEST RESULTS

At the end of Day 1, take out your journal. Fill in the appropriate time slots with the activities or tasks you plan to work on for tomorrow. Try to include as much detail as possible. Try to go slowly and put some thought into it. Now go home. Take your Time Journal with you if you are going to also assess the quality of your personal life. If not, leave it at work until tomorrow when you come back to work.

When you come to work the next day, take out the journal again as soon as you sit down. Begin to fill in the time slots on the right side of each page with what actually happened in each time slot. Try to be as accurate as possible. Take your clipboard with you wherever you go. Fill in things as they occur. Don't let it slip and then try to remember what happened all day long, only at the end of the day. It won't be very accurate.

At the end of the day, on the last page of that particular day, add up how many tasks you started and how many you completed. Pay attention to the priority of the ones you did and didn't complete.

Now repeat the same activity as you did at the end of the previous day. Turning to Day 2, fill in your plan for tomorrow. Take the

Time Journal with you and continue to keep track of your personal life that evening. Try not to omit any details.

On Days 3 through 5 continue the same procedure until you complete all five different days (Monday, Tuesday, Wednesday, Thursday, and Friday). Everyday can be very different.

When you complete all five days, put the journal away in a place you will remember. We will look at it again in greater detail once you've finished the first half of the book.

At that point you will have the skill set necessary to improve what you see in your Time Journal. The tips, tools, ideas, and strategies will definitely make more sense. You will then identify actions you can take that will save you up to two more hours a day. The results will be immediate.

Now we are ready to begin the journey of self-discovery. Once you become the Ringmaster your day will begin to change. Let's look at some ways to take more control of each day/week and your destiny.

2

Taking Control of Your Day: Becoming the Ringmaster Instead of the Beast

True prosperity is the result of well placed confidence in ourselves and our fellow man.

—BENJAMIN BURT

People have never been so reactive as they are today. Everything is instantaneous. We have more instantaneous contact with everyone we deal with (peers, friends, boss, family, clients or customers); yet the average person doesn't think he gets anything more done than he did five years ago.

In my thirteen years of research I can't find a strong correlation between instantaneous and being more productive. In fact, any gains in productivity that a cell phone and or Black Berry provide are often offset by human nature. Human nature is last in–first out. Even if we are doing something more important we will stop and respond to the new stimulus. This sets up jumping from task to task all day long. Have you ever experienced this?

Felt like you were extremely busy all day long?

When you got to the end of the day you were exhausted?

Looked on your list and discovered you still had the majority of your important work to complete?

Went home feeling a little less than fulfilled?

If you have experienced these feelings recently or seem to feel them daily, this chapter is for you. Let's look at some ways to take back control or your day and week so when you go home daily you have a feeling of true accomplishment.

YOU HAVE CHOICES

I used to complain about my peers, boss, and things that seemed to go wrong daily or weekly. I then realized that nothing was improving. I was still staying late every night and, on top of that, I was getting passed over by my peers for promotions.

One day I realized I had to become more proactive. I thought to myself, nothing is going to improve unless I do something about it. I realized that I had choices. Instead of just surviving using short-term solutions, I needed to come up with long-term solutions that made common problems permanently disappear.

An Example

My boss used to come to me (it seemed like every day) and give me a project at the end of the day. As a result I would have to stay late. I thought: What could I do about it? So I decided to stop by his office everyday around 1 p.m. to see if he had a project or task for me to complete.

One day a miracle happened, he came to my office around 1 o'clock. He said, "Before you interrupt me again, I thought I'd bring this project to you." I told him, "You don't know what this means to me!" He looked at me rather strangely. He didn't realize that I had reverse trained him.

In addition I had to ask myself if I was really showing others that I truly valued my own time by the way I was handling interruptions, new requests, deadlines, and saying yes to everyone the second they asked me for anything. I finally figured out why at the end of each day, the work I still had left on my list was mine.

Finally the Ringmaster has come to realize that his/her own actions were causing him/her to actually feel less control each day. These bad habits were:

1. Coming to work each day without a realistic plan (winging it).

2. Starting every day with 30 to 45 minutes of chit-chat with coworkers (this included getting a caffeinated beverage of some sort).

3. Opening e-mail and trying to respond to every e-mail in my in-box (regardless of priority).

4. Leaving my e-mail notification on so every time I received a new message it interrupted my thought process or what I was working on at the time.

5. Working on two to four tasks or activities at the same time until I felt like I had ADD (attention deficit disorder). I couldn't bring more that 25 percent of my focus and concentration on any one task, activity, or project.

6. Jumping from task to task all day long (the "heart patient syndrome")—phone, then e-mail, then face-to-face visit. This way I felt unfulfilled everyday when I finally went home from work because I actually finished very few tasks, activities, or projects by the end of each day. I just couldn't seem to get any momentum all day long.

7. Doing every new request I received the second I received it without asking any questions.

8. Assuming what people meant or needed.

9. Wasting time trying to figure out what the meaning of certain e-mails and/or voice mails were that were poorly written, or done too fast so you couldn't understand their call back number or meaning, or lacked certain important pieces of information.

10. Going as fast as I could for as long as possible this caused me to:

    a. Make mistakes (I had to fix).

    b. Write and speak more vaguely (which caused additional questions and misunderstandings).

    c. Ask fewer questions, even if I wasn't clear on what someone needed.

UNDERSTANDING THE RINGMASTER "MINDSET"

1. I have more control than I think.

2. I can make things improve more quickly if I take action and not wait.

3. I need to look for permanent solutions, not just Band-Aids.

4. I need to be consistent, patient, and calm.

5. I can't ever give up no matter what (I'll wear them down!).

6. I'm not going to play the "victim." No one likes a whiner or complainer.

7. I need to show others I have clear boundaries and that I respect my time.

From this point forward, picture yourself as the master of your time, masterfully controlling the beasts (interruptions, clutter, procrastination, etc.) and looking for every opportunity to take charge, slow down, and impose discipline on your chaotic environment—to take control of your day. Here are a number of Ringmaster strategies to get the "new you" started.

THE RINGMASTER'S STRATEGIES

1. Slow Down

You need to slow down. You're moving so fast that it takes multiple phone calls, e-mails, and meetings to accomplish the same thing we used to be able to do once. We have more instantaneous contact with everyone we work with, yet the average person doesn't think he gets any more done than he used to five years ago.

The faster you go:

- The less control you will feel
- The more mistakes you will make
- The more vaguely you will write or speak
- The more effort it will take to get an activity or task done (e.g., e-mail, phone call, or meeting)
- The greater the probability you are doing more than one thing at a time or incorrectly multi-tasking

The Ringmaster thinks: How can I send this e-mail once, make this call once, and/or have this meeting once and it accomplishes everything I need to get done, by when I need it, without any questions? Are you like a "machine-gun" all day long or could you be more like a "high-powered rifle" and fire one shot and be done? In order to do this you would have to:

- Plan your call before you pick up the phone.
- Plan your e-mail before you start typing.
- Prepare/give out an agenda well in advance of your meeting.

2. Defer Immediate Requests as Much as Possible

The Ringmaster considers each request on its own merit. The first thought that goes through his mind is: Is this request something I really need to do right away? The reason is because the single most, counter-productive thing you experience each day is immediacy. Immediacy causes you to jump from task to task all day long and never really complete anything meaningful.

The Ringmaster is a good listener and asks good questions about each inbound request to decide if each request really does need to be done immediately. The Ringmaster doesn't necessarily ever say "no" but rather suggests a better time in the near future so he can complete what he/she is working on and then handle the new request. By trying to defer requests the Ringmaster is trying to batch their request (see Strategy 3) with another similar activity (e.g., e-mail, phone call, or visit).

If others know they can always come to you at the last minute and get whatever they need, why should they ever plan ahead? If they know you will provide the answer or do it for them, why should they ever do it themselves?

The first time you get something for someone the moment they ask for it, what will they always expect in the future? If you deferred requests occasionally, maybe they would come to you with questions and/or requests sooner.

3. Batch Like Tasks or Activities

In order to accomplish more, the Ringmaster sets up times each day to like activities he has to accomplish to have more *discipline*. It is the second fastest way to improve productivity.

Because human nature is "last in/first out," the Ringmaster turns off the audible notification on his e-mail. Instead the Ringmaster checks his e-mail once an hour and responds to as many e-mails as possible in 10 to 15 minutes or less. Because you are only answering e-mails, each e-mail will take less time because you are basically replicating the same activity over and over. As long as you are picking the time (i.e., once an hour) to check your e-mail message you are the Ringmaster. If your e-mail goes "ding," *it* will be the Ringmaster because it will force you to respond because of human nature.

Do the same with the phone. Certain times of the day let your phone go to voice mail if you are doing something important. At least use caller ID and only answer certain calls based on the importance of the caller. Once you finish what you needed to get done, batch returning phone calls. Each call will take less time because you're only doing one activity at a time.

Finally, go see coworkers that you deferred and give them the answers to the questions they asked or the information they needed.

This strategy will prevent you from acting like a heart patient all day long (phone call, e-mail, visit, phone call, e-mail, visit, etc.). Human nature is last in/first out. Whatever impacts you last, you will try to stop what you are doing and answer the new request first. Have you ever looked at your list at the end of the day to see what you had left to accomplish and realized the answer was, *everything*? Batching like tasks will prevent this.

4. Train Others

The number one management skill today is the ability to train others. It would be great if time management were as simple as improving yourself alone. The Ringmaster realized a long time ago that even if he or she had excellent time management skills, his coworkers would still make life difficult with their poor time management skills. I had to teach others how to be more specific and brief when writing e-mails and leaving messages for me.

When someone comes to you and asks a question you should realize it is a training opportunity in disguise. If you answer their question or solve their problem quickly they will be back again (usually asking nearly the same question). Train them to come prepared to ask a question. Make them take ownership in their job or problem. Ask them:

- To clearly identify their question or problem (in writing, optional)
- What they have already tried
- What they think the answer is at that point

Offer to show them how to do it so they really learn something from your answer. Try this next time:

- First, I'll do it and you watch.
- Next, you'll do it and I'll watch.
- Finally, you are on your own.

If they can get you to do the work or answer the question, why should they ever do it themselves? People like to learn new things, but it takes time (training) to save time (long-term solution).

5. Reduce Relationship Building

One of the most important hour segments in a person's day is the first hour after he gets to work. In fact, the ways things are these days, it might be the only good hour before you lose control of your day. When you get into a groove first thing in the morning and a coworker stops by to chat, the Ringmaster suggests talking at break time or at lunch, when it's most appropriate. The Ringmaster has learned that the first hour of each day may be his only good hour. The Ringmaster tries to get something important done as soon as he gets to work, then takes a reward break to recharge.

The Ringmaster realized that relationship building was all about quality, not quantity. If you set aside time each day to share with and listen to others, the quality of your working relationships will actually improve. When you start deferring relationship building and suggest a later time, make sure you explain that you would like to hear their story but because you're so busy at the moment you can't give it the attention their story deserved.

6. Negotiate and Underpromise—Overdeliver

When the Ringmaster gets a request, he tries to fit it in where it works best for him and still works for the requestor. If the requestor needed something, I would ask, "Can I get that to you by the end of the day?" I would then try to get what they needed to them much earlier. By setting their expectation to the end of the day, people are always happy when they get what they needed sooner. Be sure you write down their request so you don't let them down and forget to do it by when you promised. The Ringmaster's word is his bond!

When you drop what you're doing and handle a request the moment it's made, it's 90 percent in their favor and 10 percent in your favor. All you really want is 50/50. By deferring his request you can batch their request with something similar you'll be doing in the near future.

7. Change Your Voice Mail Greeting Daily or Weekly

The Ringmaster changes his voice mail greeting daily or weekly and asks callers to leave their name, number, reason for their call, and the best time to call them back. He/she explains that if they do that, he/she will call them back more quickly with the help or information the requestor needs and if necessary leave it on their voice mail. This strategy will also cut down on phone tag. Without knowing why they are calling, how can you prioritize returning their voice mail message?

After that, if the requestor continues to leave poor messages, the Ringmaster doesn't try to figure it out. He waits for them to call again. This is called "reinforcing" your request. People are willing to modify their behavior if they see what's in it for them. Do you really want to play phone tag all day long?

You must lead by example. When you leave messages for others, you must leave your name, number, reason for your call, and the best time for them to call you back. Remember, leave your phone number twice and don't speak too quickly.

8. Improve the Quality of the E-mail You Receive

Do you waste time each day trying to figure out the reason or meaning of many of the e-mails you receive? Do you get e-mails that don't even have a subject line? The Ringmaster has learned it is in his best interests to train others how to write him e-mails so it would save him time reading and responding to each one. Ask others to:

- Put the reason they're sending an e-mail to you in the subject line.
- Put what they want or need in the first three lines of the message.
- Keep their first paragraph to no more than two to three lines long so it fits into the Preview Pane in Outlook or Lotus Notes. (Explain that you don't typically open all the e-mails you receive because you get so many.) That is why you typically prioritize opening and responding to e-mails based on the quality of each subject line and first paragraph only.
- Put their specific deadline in the subject line (if their request is time sensitive) so you see their request immediately.

- Use numbers or bullets instead of long sentences and/or paragraphs when they need more than one thing or have more than one question so their request is easier and faster to respond to. Explain it will save you time by putting the answer after each of their numbers or bullets.

- Tell you when they need an answer by and why (urgency and importance) at the end of their e-mail so you can accurately prioritize their request. Explain if they did that you could respond faster to their e-mail messages. If they continue to write you poor e-mail messages, responses are going to take longer.

You need to write your e-mail this way for others first and be an example. That way, next time they hit the reply key, they may follow your example. To see this writing model in detail, see pages 94–95 where you will also find the "PADD" model (see Chapter 7). It will save you time writing and reading other's e-mails.

TIP: I also use the PADD model (see Chapter 7) to organize my phone calls before I pick up the phone. This model makes it easier and faster to organize your thoughts *before* you begin to write or talk, and it makes it clearer and more logical for the reader or listener to understand.

9. Direct the Request to the Right Person

Are you a people pleaser? When the Ringmaster gets a request that is not in his area of expertise, he directs the requestor to the right person. He doesn't try to become an expert on the spot. It is faster for the right person to answer the question or solve the problem than it is for you to try.

10. Improve Your Communication Skills

The Ringmaster possesses excellent communication skills. One of the fastest ways to improve productivity is to be more specific and detailed with others. This will save time for you and others. This really eliminates questions and misunderstandings.

Being vague may save you time initially when you write the e-mail or leave the voice mail message, but it usually costs you more time in the long run. That's why you need to plan your e-mail message before you begin writing and plan your phone call before you pick up the phone. Planning always saves time.

11. Focus on One Thing at a Time—Go for Completion

The Ringmaster is a "traffic cop" who directs the flow of work that comes across his desk every day. Think of a typical traffic cop. He stands in an intersection, motioning for cars in one direction to move forward into the intersection and the others to stay where they are.

Now imagine what you look like every day. Is it safe to say that you're motioning in all four directions? You could handle traffic more effectively if it was coming from one direction at a time. Try to bring 100 percent of your focus and concentration to bear on one activity. Tasks will take less time to complete and you'll make fewer mistakes. Either chose the phone call or the e-mail message, and put off the other until you've finished the one you chose.

3

Using a Master List to Create a Plan That Works: Developing an Effective Master List to Organize Everything You Need to Get Done

If you wish to forget something on the spot, make a note that this thing is to be remembered.

—EDGAR ALLEN POE

USING A MASTER LIST TO CREATE A PLAN THAT WORKS

The new tools recommended here are not traditional to-do lists. Rather, they are the two key building blocks of staying organized—on a daily, weekly, monthly, and annual basis—the Master List and the Daily List. In brief, a Master List is a pad of paper where you will keep all the possible activities, notes, action items, and so on for an entire week. Have you ever seen a football coach on the sidelines either on a Saturday or Sunday? They have a laminated sheet they look at with all the possible plays they could call, all in one place. That is the principle here.

A Daily List is an electronic calendar where you will plan a realistic number of key activities for that day only. Together, the Master List and the Daily List replace the traditional to-do list and day planner. The material that follows explains these lists in detail and how to make the best use of them in combination with your calendar or an electronic organizer system.

HOW TO CREATE AND USE A MASTER LIST

1. The purpose of a Master List is to get everything out of your head. A Master List is a *journal* of thoughts and activities as they occur. The mind can organize what you need to accomplish more effectively when it can see everything you need to complete.

2. A to-do list is a list that is done daily and mainly focuses on that specific day. Since a Master List is a journal of random thoughts as they occur, you will be writing down tasks or activities that aren't necessarily to be done that day. This brain storming process will allow your mind to think ahead into the future. If you want to "get ahead of the curve," you need to start considering and working on the future now before it becomes the present.

   Every time you have a thought, idea, make a request, or receive a request, write it down right away.

3. The Master List is only rewritten once a week. Why make a new list every day? It's a waste of time. A weekly time frame is a better indication of your productivity than a single day. Each week you may have a bad day or two in terms of what you accomplished but if you looked at all five days you will probably see you did pretty well and not be so discouraged. If you consider a football game, one team doesn't win because they had one good quarter. They won because at the end of four quarters they had the higher score. It is the same principle here.

4. The Master List is saved each week, stapled together, and put in a file; it is used as backup from time to time, and at the end of the year to complete your review. This will allow you to jog other's memory when they forget they told you something. In addition, the average person rarely gets the credit her/she deserves because they can't remember all of the significant tasks, projects, and bonus activities they did that year. By looking back through your saved Master Lists at the end of the year you can underline or highlight the events that support why you deserve a raise or promotion. The Ringmaster is always educating his/her boss as to how indispensible her/she is. The Master List provides very visual proof. Don't throw away the "evidence" each day.

5. Skip lines between each entry to leave room to make notes and add details. Also, it will make it easier to find details you are looking for quickly.

6. Use the double-wide margin for phone numbers, e-mail addresses, and as a "quick find" for a note to the right. Have you noticed most pads you find in stationary stores are actually writing tablets? They only have a one inch margin which isn't very useful.

7. If you have to leave a voice mail or send an e-mail, give yourself a check mark but put a circle around it. Don't fill in your circle until you receive a return call or e-mail, then fill it in. This will make you a great "squeaky wheel" and deadly on follow-up. At the end of the day, before you go home if that circle around your check mark is still empty, follow-up up again with them. If your request is very time sensitive, keep following up with them at least daily until

they call you back or e-mail you with the answer you needed. You are going to train them that you can keep track of that loose end longer than they can avoid calling or e-mailing you back. You are training them.

8. Don't prioritize your Master List. Make a detailed short note so you can tell the priority of what you wrote down. This will keep your list flexible, because your day and priorities are constantly changing.

Everytime you complete one task, look through your Master List and use these criteria to reset your priorities and determine the best use of your time at that moment. The critiera are:

- How much time do I have available? Are you looking to fill 10, 30, or 60 minutes?

- How much energy do you have at this moment? How fresh are you? (If you have a lot of energy you can pick a difficult task, if you are tired maybe an easy task like e-mail might be a better fit.

- Based on time available and your energy level, now pick the task that best fits from your Master List.

  By using this process you can constantly reset your priorities and stay flexible as your day is changing.

9. If the request has a deadline, write the date in the box marked "date due" and move it to your electronic calendar at your first opportunity.

10. Make sure the first word of each note you write tells you what the activity is. For example, e-mail Bill, call Susan, and go see Mary, or pay bills tonight. This process sets up batching like tasks.

11. Make sure your Master List includes not only to-do tasks but also

- Notes from conversations
- Ideas
- Things you don't want to forget
- Personal to-dos
- Tasks with deadlines to add to your calendar
- Meeting notes with action items separated out so you don't forget to do them

12. Only have one list. One list is easy to manage. With a Master List, everything is in one place. Most people have multiple to-do lists in the form of loose paper or Post-its. Your Master List must be very portable because you need to take it with you everywhere you go. Your mind is constantly in the "on" position. You never know when a great thought or item not to forget will pop into your head. The mind is very random. Don't have one list for home and one list for work. Combine them both into one so it is easier to maintain your list.

NOTE: On the following page is a sample of a Master List so you can visually see the concept and how to do this activity.

Activity

Take out a pad or piece of paper. For the next 10 minutes write down any ideas, don't forgets, or to-do tasks that pop into your head in no particular order. Don't forget your personal life items. Be sure you skip a line in between each item. Before you leave work today or at the end of your day please update what you wrote down with additional thoughts, e-mails, phone calls, and don't forgets.

Sample Master List

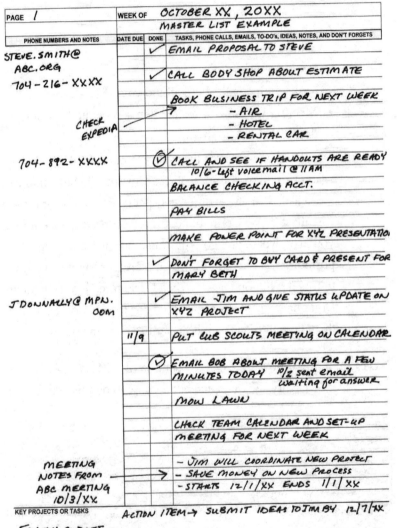

PAGE 1	WEEK OF	OCTOBER XX, 20XX
		MASTER LIST EXAMPLE
PHONE NUMBERS AND NOTES	**DATE DUE** | **DONE**	**TASKS, PHONE CALLS, EMAILS, TO-DO's, IDEAS, NOTES, AND DON'T FORGETS**

STEVE.SMITH@ ABC.ORG
704-216-XXXX

✓ EMAIL PROPOSAL TO STEVE

✓ CALL BODY SHOP ABOUT ESTIMATE

BOOK BUSINESS TRIP FOR NEXT WEEK
    - AIR
    - HOTEL
    - RENTAL CAR

CHECK EXPEDIA

704-892-XXXX

Ⓥ CALL AND SEE IF HANDOUTS ARE READY
10/6 - Left voicemail @ 11 AM

BALANCE CHECKING ACCT.

PAY BILLS

MAKE POWER POINT FOR XYZ PRESENTATION

✓ DON'T FORGET TO BUY CARD & PRESENT FOR MARY BETH

JDONNALLY@MPN.COM

✓ EMAIL JIM AND GIVE STATUS UPDATE ON XYZ PROJECT

11/9   PUT CUB SCOUTS MEETING ON CALENDAR

Ⓥ EMAIL BOB ABOUT MEETING FOR A FEW MINUTES TODAY 10/2 sent email waiting for answer

MOW LAWN

CHECK TEAM CALENDAR AND SET-UP MEETING FOR NEXT WEEK

MEETING NOTES FROM ABC MEETING 10/3/XX →
   - JIM WILL COORDINATE NEW PROJECT
   - SAVE MONEY ON NEW PROCESS
   - STARTS 12/1/XX ENDS 1/1/XX

KEY PROJECTS OR TASKS   ACTION ITEM → SUBMIT IDEAS TO JIM BY 12/7/XX

FINISH BUDGET
MAKE CAR PAYMENT
WORK ON MARKETING PROJECT

QUICK TIPS

✓ Have only one list. Get rid of the Post-its, multiple pads of paper, scrap paper. Experiment until you find a single pad that you like (electronic or paper). The purpose of a Master List is to keep your mind as empty as possible so you'll be less overwhelmed.

✓ As you make commitments or as ideas pop into your head, write them down to keep your brain free (so it can react faster).

✓ Skip lines in between each entry so you can make notes and find specific notes faster.

✓ Don't prioritize your list the night before. Wait until after you check your e-mail and voice mail first thing in the morning.

✓ Accept the reality that you're not going to get everything done today.

✓ Make sure your Master List is portable so you can take it everywhere.

✓ A Master List goes from Friday to Friday. You typically only rewrite it once a week (unless it gets too large). If organizing takes too long, you'll stop doing it. Keep your list simple.

✓ File your Master Lists each week and save them for your annual review and for back-up in case there is a disagreement or someone doesn't remember.

✓ A typical Master List will be 10 to 20 pages a week depending on how much you write down each day. The more you write down, the more you'll accomplish.

✓ Use a double-wide margin so you have extra room for phone numbers, e-mail addresses, and important information, so you can find them more quickly.

✓ Use a check mark and a circle around the check mark to denote a task you've done but you're waiting for an answer or completion.

✓ If a task, activity, or project has a specific deadline, write it on your Master List right away then transfer it to your calendar when you get a moment.

✓ Without a Master List you have a 90 percent chance of doing every request the moment you receive one, because your mind says, "I better do it now or I'll forget to do it later."

✓ Use your Master List to defer requests, then batch similar tasks to save time.

✓ When you agree to do something at a later time or date, write it down immediately, because your word is your bond.

✓ Make sure you put your personal life on your Master List so you don't forget to have one. It will improve the quality and quantity of your personal life.

4

Organizing and Planning a More Effective Day and Week

It is more important to know where you are going than to get there quickly. Do not mistake activity for achievement.

—MABEL NEWCOMER

USING THE END OF YOUR DAY TO INCREASE YOUR PRODUCTIVITY

Productivity improvement actually starts with how you finish each day. Do you think about work at night or wake up in a cold sweat? Many times the cause of this is the mind is very uncomfortable with the unknown. When you leave work with unresolved issues or at loose ends, the mind is bound to think about it. Maybe you can't increase the amount of personal time you have daily and weekly, but wouldn't you like to improve the quality of it by being mentally and emotionally available to others when you got home? We need to turn the lights off mentally when we leave work.

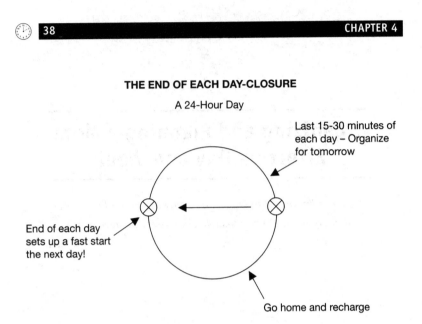

THE END OF EACH DAY-CLOSURE

A 24-Hour Day

Last 15-30 minutes of each day – Organize for tomorrow

End of each day sets up a fast start the next day!

Go home and recharge

THE FIRST KEY TO PRODUCTIVITY IS HOW YOU END EACH DAY—THE END OF EACH DAY IS THE SPRINGBOARD FOR GETTING OFF TO A FAST START THE NEXT DAY

1. A Master List is updated at the end of each day. Fifteen to 30 minutes before you plan to leave work, stop responding to e-mails, phone calls, requests from others, and your work. This is your time. With your calendar open and your Master List in front of you, let your mind wander. Brainstorm: write down whatever pops into your head in particular order. Why do it at the end of every day? Here are some reasons:

   • Closure

   • It's still fresh in your mind. How much do you remember the next day when you plan the following morning?

- Mental separation between work and home. Maybe you can't increase the amount of personal time you have but you could improve the quality of it!

- Time and a place for everything. Organizing is perfect when your energy level is low at the end of the day because organizing doesn't take a lot of energy. You don't want to start you day organizing when you are fresh and ready to go with good energy.

- So you can use the evening to recharge and get ready for tomorrow.

- People look forward to coming to work more the next day when they come to work and they already have a plan.

- If you come to work without a Master List you will have a very high probability you'll open e-mail and get bogged down. If you have a Master List from the day before, when you look at your list you'll see that what you already have on your list is probably a higher priority than the new tasks or requests you get first thing in the morning via e-mail. Thus you will increase your discipline to focus on what matters most first before your day gets out of control.

At the end of the day, the concept is that:

- An idea pops into your head.
- You write it down.
- Then you delete the thought from your brain.

By planning the night before, you'll have about 75 percent of the picture. You won't be able to fill in the rest of the picture until you see the requests waiting for you in e-mail and on your voice mail. Then you can prioritize and get started.

You need to plan the night before and develop a plan that's very flexible and can change at a minute's notice; otherwise, you'll go back to flying by the seat of your pants. That's how people become a product of their environment and their day. Without a plan the chances of your day taking control of you greatly increase. Everything small and urgent will take the place of everything that matters most.

2. When you come to work the next day you will be adding to and crossing off tasks on your Master List all day long. Capture new items and tasks on your Master List as soon as you're given them or they pop into your head.

3. Accept the reality that not everything will get crossed off your list each day or weekly. This is going to be a big list and the purpose of the list is not to get them all crossed off. At the end of the day, you just want to see you got done what you really needed to get done. In other words, based on the circumstances you faced all day long, did you make the best use of your time throughout the day? If you can say yes, you had a pretty good day!

4. Keep your list with you at all times. You're always getting and or giving new requests from or to others and coming up with new ideas. Your Master List must be very portable, so you will take it with you wherever you go.

GET OF TO A FASTER START EACH DAY!

A 24-Hour Day

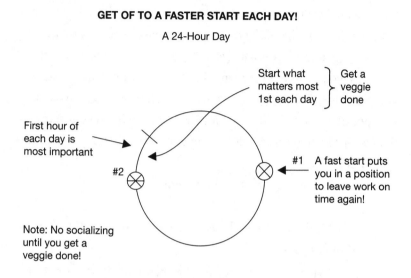

THE SECOND KEY TO PRODUCTIVITY IS HOW YOU START EACH DAY—USING THE VEGGIE PRINCIPLE TO FOCUS ON WHAT MATTERS MOST

This is the most important principle in the book. A "veggie" is a task, activity, or project that's good for you, your career, or personal life but that you have a hard time "eating," or doing first. Without the benefit of training such as this, people will typically start working on a veggie late in the day or evening when they are less effective.

The true secret to getting the right tasks accomplished at the right time is to apply the veggie principle, that is, tackle first in the day those action items that directly impact your highest goals and priorities. What you accomplish in the first hour of each day is the second key to increasing your productivity. The first hour of your day may be the only good hour you have before you lose control of your day. If you can get a veggie done in the first hour of your day you have a 90 percent chance of leaving work on time (if you want to). Following the veggie principle will save you time, improve end results, reduce procrastination, and build your self-confidence. The veggie principle is a thought process. I use it in everything I do.

Here are some examples of how I use it:

1. At work, I start with the most difficult task that has the highest payoff.
2. At home (when I get home at night or on the weekend), I work on the task I like the least so I can enjoy the rest of the night or weekend.
3. When I create a meeting agenda, I address the most important issues or topics first, so that if I run out of time, everyone can still leave the meeting on time.

GET MORE DONE BY 12 NOON!

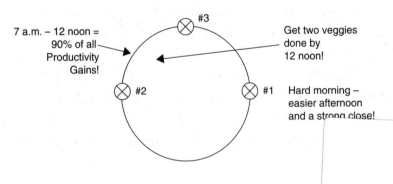

THE THIRD KEY TO PRODUCTIVITY IS HOW MUCH YOU GET DONE BY NOON

About 90 percent of all productivity gains occur between 7 a.m. and 12 p.m. If your day doesn't follow that typical schedule, you would look for your gains in the first half of you day or shift. The problem is not the afternoon. How could you move the pressure to the first half or your day when you are fresher and more focused?

TIP: The concept is to figure out how can you match up when you are best mentally/physically against the toughest, most important tasks you need to complete each day.

MAKING AN EFFECTIVE DAILY LIST

After you finish updating your Master List at the end of the day, select the two most important tasks and put them on your electronic or paper calendar for tomorrow. To increase the chances you will work on them the next day, block off time on your computer to get them done. This will increase your commitment to getting those important tasks done. (Only block off one hour increments and make sure they aren't back to back.) Remember, you need to leave time each hour to batch responding to e-mail, returning phone calls, and face-to-face requests and/or interaction.

KEY POINT: It's better to under promise and over deliver. Say to yourself, "No matter what, I'm going to accomplish two veggies today." Then, try to get 10 done. This will help you prevent yourself from going home with a feeling you didn't accomplish anything that day. (Many people plan too many tasks and get nothing done. Have you ever left work and left a little less than fulfilled? It is better to make plans based on a typical chaotic, difficult day than a perfect day that doesn't ever happen.)

How many items you put into your plan for tomorrow depends on what you already have scheduled (meetings, deadlines, and prior commitments, etc.). Your list will also depend on how much control you have over your day.

When you come in first thing in the morning, if you start with two from the night before, you'll probably find two or three more activities in your e-mail and two or three important voice mails. Now you're up to six to eight tasks or activities, and that's a full day's work.

TIP: When you open e-mail messages and listen to voice mail first thing in the morning, you're only looking for veggies. A veggie e-mail or voice mail must have a specific deadline to be done immediately and say why it's so critical you do it right away. Otherwise, you are going to defer on returning most e-mail and voice mail requests until after you complete your first veggie. Compare those e-mails and voice mails to what you already have on your list from the night before. Typically, you'll see that what you already had on your list is more important than the new requests you receive first thing in the morning.

Now, place a star next to the two biggest veggies on your list. Typically, the top two will give you 80 percent of the value of all the tasks on your list together. The trick is to honestly identify the two biggest tasks, using the veggie principle. Try to start your day with one of these two, and complete the other before lunch. Don't leave them for the afternoon.

HOW TO PUT TOGETHER A POWERFUL MORNING

When I look at the Timekeeping Journals people keep, I focus on the first hour of each day to see what kind of start they're getting off to. Most of the time, the average person gets very little accomplished besides e-mail.

The average person spends one to three hours:

- Checking e-mail
- Responding to voice mail and the phone
- Handling drop-by visitors and their immediate requests
- Checking in with others, checking in with their boss, or relationship building

TIP: This time slot needs to be cut down to 15 to 30 minutes so you can start your first veggie more quickly. This is how to use the veggie principle to your advantage and gain discipline so you get more done before lunch.

Here's a new way to start every day and get more done in the morning. Let's say you start your day at 8 a.m.:

8:00–8:15   When you check e-mail and voice mail first,
                     only look for veggies. Compare the e-mails
                     and phone messages first thing in the morning
                     to the veggies you already have scheduled
                     from the night before. If you see any veggies,
                     complete them, add other requests to your
                     list, close e-mail, put the phone on voice mail,
                     and jump into your list. Turn off your e-mail
                     notification.

8:15–9:15   Work on your biggest veggie, or most impor-
                     tant task. This slot is one hour. Try to defer
                     any interruptions that come your way during
                     this hour. Ask them if you could get back to
                     them shortly, as soon as your veggie time
                     is over.

9:15–10:15   Complete your veggie and check e-mail, listen
                     to voice mail, and allow interruptions. Look
                     for the veggies and respond to them as quickly
                     as possible. Allow 60 minutes to complete as
                     many requests as possible.

10:15–11:15   As soon as you're done, close your e-mail, put
                     the phone back on voice mail, and try to defer
                     interruptions for the next short block of time.
                     Go to the second biggest veggie and try to
                     work on it for 60 minutes.

11:15–11:30   After you finish veggie 2, return lower prior-
                     ity e-mails and phone calls. Get back under

control before you go to lunch. You will notice that people are very quick with you during this time slot (that's the idea).

11:30–12:15   Schedule in a lunch break so you stay fresh for the afternoon. Remember, don't work and eat at the same time. Both will take more time and you won't do either well.

TIP: Remember to take lunch opposite your biggest interrupters. While they're at lunch, it will be quiet and you can get veggie 3 done. When they come back from lunch, you can go. It makes for a shorter afternoon.

Move Meetings to the Afternoon

There are three types of meetings:

- Informational
- Decision-making
- Brainstorming

The meeting has to be a veggie meeting to be scheduled in the morning. In other words the meeting should only be scheduled in the morning if a decision is required or you are trying to come up with high quality ideas. Informational or status meetings should be moved to the afternoon. If your morning gets filled up with meetings, how are you ever going to get any veggies done?

Use Your Energy Cycles to Your Advantage

Everyone has at least three energy cycles in a day. For 75 percent of us, the strongest cycle is the morning, the next strongest in the afternoon, and the weakest in the evening. Why does the one in the evening (while you're still at work) often seem the best? Maybe because everyone else has gone home and you don't have any interruptions.

That's why you need to "protect" your "primo" time in the morning. Some suggestions would be to avoid meetings, turn off e-mail, and let phone calls go to voice mail. Block off the first hour of each day on your Outlook calendar so you can get at least one veggie done each day.

It took me a long time to realize that others were taking advantage of my best time to get things done. They were reducing my most productive time of the day to a "pimple," and I was letting them. When I didn't use the morning to my advantage, it forced key tasks and projects into the afternoon when I was less effective. My projects took more time to accomplish and I ended up having to stay late.

Have a Group Power Hour

Get together with your team or group and pick an hour each morning (that everyone could agree to) and agree to limit:

- Face-to-face interruptions
- Noise (loud talking)
- Relationship building

- Speakerphones
- Non-essential questions

Everyone agree to focus on a veggie and see what they can get done in an hour with limited interruptions. It's a team thing and will become a source of camaraderie. When the power hour ends then take a break and see how much everyone got done. (You will be amazed!)

Stop Working Late at Night

There has been a dramatic increase in the number of people working late at night. Stop sneaking over to your computer to check and send e-mail or work on things you didn't get done that day. You're only putting pressure on your morning cycle. The later you work, the harder it will be to bring your "A" game first thing in the morning. Eventually the cycle will turn against you and you will go from being a "morning" person, to an "afternoon" person in terms of when you are productive.

When you consistently work late at night, you start to build that cushion into your schedule and reduce your sense of urgency to get more done earlier in the day. If you eliminate the option of working at home late at night, the morning becomes significantly more important. Remember the saying: there's a time and a place for everything. Ask yourself, "How can I get more done by noon so I don't have to work at home tonight?"

A final consideration is that the more tired you become, or run-down at work, eventually the slower you will work and the chance of procrastination will increase.

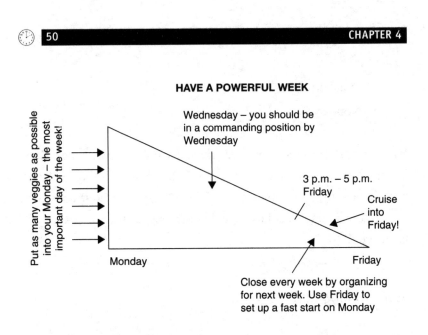

HAVE A POWERFUL WEEK

Put as many veggies as possible into your Monday – the most important day of the week!

Wednesday – you should be in a commanding position by Wednesday

3 p.m. – 5 p.m. Friday

Cruise into Friday!

Monday

Friday

Close every week by organizing for next week. Use Friday to set up a fast start on Monday

HOW TO PUT TOGETHER A MORE PRODUCTIVE AND POWERFUL WEEK

This concept will seem very similar to setting up a more effective day. Setting up a more productive week actually starts with how you end the week. This will have an impact on your weekend and how fast a start you get off to the following Monday. The principle is how can you make Monday your most difficult day of your week (a pure veggie day), be in a commanding position by Wednesday, and cruise into the end of the day on Friday? Let's look at some strategies for improving what you accomplish each week.

Plan the Following Week on Friday

Friday is a much underutilized day. It is the best day for organizing. It is the springboard for the following week.

Here are some benefits of choosing Friday afternoon to organize:

- You can review the current week while you're still in it and it's still fresh in your mind. You can assess what you accomplished and what needs to move to next week and on what day.

- You can reflect on:

  a. A job well done

  b. What changes you'll make next week

  c. What you could have done differently

  d. Why a certain task didn't get done

- All the checkmarks (which makes it easier to enjoy the weekend). When your plan for next week and Monday is specifically down on paper, you don't have to spend the weekend worrying. You'll gain a sense of confidence that things are "under control."

- Friday afternoon is one of the least productive times of the week. By Friday afternoon, we begin to turn our attention to the weekend but even this time is just right for one particular task. Friday afternoon is a perfect time to reload for next week. Not only plan next week, but also delete e-mails, throw away paper, file, and clean off your desk. Get ready for the big push on Monday.

- The game really runs Friday to Friday. On Friday, I'm only going to transfer to next week the tasks I didn't complete this week. I also ask, "If I didn't get this high-priority task done this week, what am I going to do differently next week to complete it?" This is a great way to improve each week.

- For mental closure so I can stop thinking about work all weekend, recharge, and enjoy my weekend. That way I'll be fresher on Monday morning so I can get off to a faster start.

I used to end every week on a dead run. When I decided to "front-end" load my week (start working on my most difficult tasks on Monday, not Friday), everything changed. I tried to make the beginning part of the week very difficult and tried to "cruise" into Friday. Now, I'm basically done with my week by 2 to 3 p.m. on Friday, so I can use the rest of the day to:

- Make a new Master List for next week. Only transfer items you didn't complete this week to your new Master List.
- File the Master List from your current week.
- Clean off the top of my desk (add to-dos to your Master List and file; or if you didn't look at it this week, throw it away).
- Clean out your e-mail in-box:
  - File (Set an electronic reminder or put it on your Master List.)
  - Delete (If you didn't read it this week, what are the chances you'll read it next week?)
  - Respond and file or delete after responding

Make Monday Morning Critical and Get Off to a Fast Start

Monday sets the tone for the week. If you get off to a fast start Monday, chances are the rest of the week will be easier and flow better. Make Monday morning your most powerful time by getting the most difficult work out of the way first, then cruise into Friday. A poor start could mean a poor week.

TIP: If you get to work early only one day a week, make sure it's Monday. Sometimes I get into work at 6 a.m. on Mondays just to be sure that a difficult week gets off to a fast start.

TIP: Don't schedule staff meetings or conference calls first thing Monday morning, or any morning for that matter. They just kill everyone's productivity and rob them of their best energy cycle. Try moving staff meetings to the end of the week. The purpose of the meeting is to review the progress of the team or department that week and get everyone on the same page for next week.

Get to Work Early and Leave on Time

It's better to get to work early and leave on time than to get to work on time and leave late. You should be looking for balance. Most families are much more aware of when you come home late from work than if you leave home early. It's very difficult to have a personal life when you're always coming home late.

In addition, most people are morning people. Take advantage of that. Also set an example of already being there when others start arriving. When you get there, it's quieter and maybe you can get something important done before everyone else gets there.

Start Your Morning the Night Before

Think of all the tasks that you could do the night before to make the morning easier and more routine. A few ideas:

- Select what you're going to wear tomorrow; iron it ahead of time.
- If you have children, prepare and pack their lunches that night.
- Set the timer on the coffeepot.
- Put the items you're going to take to work by the door.
- Make sure your car has gas.
- What could you add to this list? This is a major area that causes people to be late and make excuses when they get to work. It also causes their day to get off to a very stressful start. Can you get into a groove before work starts?

Don't Over Plan Your Day—Leave Room for the Unexpected

Studies show that the average person can only plan 25 to 50 percent of his day. We tend to underestimate, on the average, by 20 percent the time a task will take. As a result, day after day, we fill every time slot in our day planners and at the end of each day, it can take up to an hour just moving everything to the next day.

It's as if we're telling ourselves that we're not going to have any interruptions, the phone won't ring with an urgent request, there won't be any meetings scheduled at the last minute, and everything is going to flow smoothly all day long. Accept, instead, that this is going to be a typically busy day and put it into your plan.

Use Breaks and Lunch to Keep Your Mind Fresh Throughout the Day

It's important to keep your mind fresh throughout the day. The mind can only go so long before it "hits the wall." That's why lunch and short breaks are important. Studies show that concentration cycles usually last 90 minutes. After 90 minutes, take a 10-minute break and recharge. Perhaps do an easy, personal, or enjoyable task on your Master List or get something to drink. This will keep you fresh and reduce the chances of procrastination. Eat a lunch that will add to your afternoon energy cycle, not put you to sleep. If you have a heavy lunch, that will defeat the purpose of using lunch to increase your productivity.

QUICK TIPS

✓ Block off the last 15 to 20 minutes daily to get as much as you can out of your head and onto paper, while it's still fresh on your mind, so you can put closure on the day.

✓ Organizing is best done at the end of each day when you're tired. By moving this activity from the beginning of each day to the end of the previous day, you will be able to get a veggie done each day in the first hour.

✓ Focus on your family at night because you need time to recharge so you can get off to a fast start the next morning.

✓ When you come to work the next day, add new requests to the end of your list and cross off existing tasks or activities as you complete them.

✓ Accept the reality that not everything is going to get completed on your Master List by the end of each day or week. That's not the purpose of a Master List. At the end of everyday you just want to be sure that you did the best you could, based on the factors you faced each day and that week.

✓ Take your Master List with you wherever you go. The mind is always thinking and reacting. If you don't write it down the first time you think of something, what are the chances you'll remember that great idea again?

✓ Think of ways to apply the veggie principle to everything you do.

✓ Start every day with a veggie.

✓ Try to get two veggies done before noon. (Put more pressure on yourself to accomplish more before noon.)

✓ Block off time each day to get important tasks and projects done.

✓ Negotiate the fires around your veggies so they won't overwhelm what matters most.

✓ Have a more effective Daily List (electronic calendar) by focusing on completing two veggies, then go back and complete more. If you focus on too many tasks, you won't get any of them done each day.

✓ Don't start each day relationship building. Don't socialize each day until you get a veggie done first.

✓ Use your energy cycles to your advantage. Do difficult, high pay-off tasks when you have the most energy, and do easy tasks when you are tired.

✓ Set up times to batch e-mail and phone calls so they'll take less time.

✓ Prepare for tomorrow morning (before work) the night before.

✓ Get to work early and leave on time. Stop working late or at home.

5

Prioritizing and Giving Others Your Priorities

You seldom get what you go after unless you know in advance what you want. Indecision has often given an advantage to the other fellow because he did his thinking beforehand.

—MAURICE SWITZER

WHY WE HAVE TROUBLE PRIORITIZING ACCURATELY

The three biggest reasons why people have trouble prioritizing quickly and accurately are:

1. They try to prioritize without the essential information needed. As you will see, the fastest way to improve how you prioritize is to ask better questions.

2. They let human nature get in the way, so they work on what they'd rather work on instead of what they know (deep down) they should work on.

3. They are given very little information at the time the request is made.

HOW HUMAN NATURE AFFECTS THE WAY WE PRIORITIZE

Oftentimes, we have all the best intentions. We look at our to-do list and select the next activity we're going to work on. Was it or wasn't it the right task? When we are brutally honest, we realize that many times we picked the wrong task. Have you ever reached the end of the day, looked down at your list, and the only tasks left were your veggies? As a great procrastinator, it took me a long time to realize how human nature played a role in how I prioritized. It wasn't until I became honest that my prioritization improved and I began to work on my veggies more often than not.

Do Any of These Characteristics Look Familiar?

- We do things we enjoy first.
- We do easy tasks or requests first.
- We do requests or tasks that don't take a lot of time.
- We like to wait until the last minute to start tasks, projects, and goals.
- We like to work on tasks that interest us (because they seem like they take less time).
- We work on the last interruption first and drop what we're currently doing (no matter how important it is).
- We like to work on things we know how to do first and wait on others that need information or training.
- We start small tasks before ones that look large (and difficult).

- We'd rather do others' requests before our own veggie.
- The task selection is often based on habit, not clear thought.

Now that you're aware of the role human nature plays in how you pick your tasks, you need to slow down and consider your motivation for picking certain tasks. The faster you select and complete the tasks that relate to your goals, your boss, and your key projects, the sooner you can go home every day.

DETERMINING AND HANDLING PRIORITIES

The first step in establishing priorities is keeping track of your time for a week, both at work and at home. Very few people step back and look at what they're really doing with their time. Many become products of their environment; they just seem to "go with the flow."

When I took an honest look at my Timekeeping Journal, I realized I was part of the problem and needed to improve the information I was receiving when tasks and projects were given to me. I realized it was faster to ask questions than to guess or assume the right answer. Remember that when you make assumptions, it takes longer and you have a 50 percent chance of being wrong. Why not improve your odds?

(If you have not already completed the Timekeeping Journal, now would be an excellent time to do so. Everyone who does this exercise has unexpected insights from it that motivate them to develop their organizational skills.)

ESTABLISHING PRIORITIES

There are two ways to prioritize:

- The traditional A, B, C prioritizing approach
- The new Best Use of Your Time approach

Today people either use some sort of decision-making matrix, or just guess based on who's asking for something or what their position is at the company. I am going to show you ways to improve the speed and accuracy of your prioritizing.

The Traditional A, B, C Prioritizing Approach

A priorities are must-do tasks that have today as a specific deadline to be completed. They should

- Be important to your leader.
- Offer visibility for you and your skills.
- Be vital to the needs of your customer, peers, or team members.

B priorities are should-do tasks. These are also veggies but don't have today as a specific deadline. As you plan more effectively, these are the tasks you want to work on before they become A priorities.

C priorities are would-like-to-do tasks. These are to be worked on and completed whenever you have extra time.

TIP: The key difference between an A priority and a B priority is that an A priority has a specific deadline to be done today and a B priority has a specific deadline further out than today.

The New Best Use of Your Time Approach to Prioritizing

Every time you complete a task, before you start another one, take out your Master List and consider these three factors before you select what you work on next:

1. How much time do you have available? If you only say have 10 to 15 minutes you may not have enough time to start a project. A better use of this time might be return three phone calls or respond to two e-mails.

2. How much energy do you have? Is this your peak energy cycle or are you worn out? If you are fresh, a veggie would be a perfect choice. If you are tired, maybe responding to e-mails would be a better fit.

3. What is the highest priority task you can fit into this time frame? If you only have a short period of time, maybe doing a piece of a project would be a good fit so you can keep that project moving. If you have more time, maybe a larger part of that project could fit.

How to Determine the Correct Priority (Urgency versus Importance)

1. If you get a vague deadline like "as soon as possible" (ASAP), you must ask, "When do you really need it?"

Otherwise, how would you know how to prioritize it against your existing work? *When you know the specific deadline, you then know the correct "urgency" of the request.*

2. You need to know the reason, or why, a request is so important. Ask questions to determine if the request is really that important. *When you know why they needs their request done by a specific time, you then know why their request is so important.*

TIP: Have you ever rushed to get a task done for someone because they said they needed it ASAP, only to find out days later they hadn't even started working on the information you sent them? That's why it's so important to find out why they need a request done by a certain time.

The reason what I just showed you is so important is because one day I realized why everything on my list was an A priority. It was because everyone said their request was urgent and important. Well, under the Traditional Approach, that would make their request an A priority. After I asked the questions, "When to you really need it by?" and found out why they needed it by that specific time, I discovered at least 50 percent of the time their request wasn't an A priority after all.

The Decision-Making Matrix

Time Sensitive Veggie (A)	Not Due Today Veggie (B)
Time Sensitive Master List (C)	Whenever I Can (If I have spare time)

Everything on the left side of the matrix has to be done today, while everything on the right does not. (This is why a specific deadline is so important.)

TIP: To plan more effectively, you should be working on tasks in the upper right-hand box every day so they don't end up in the upper left-hand box. That's how you start to get "ahead of the curve": by working on tasks a little every day, before they're due.

A CASE STUDY

Jim's workload seemed very difficult. Everything seemed like it should receive the same priority. At times, he prioritized by who bothered him the most, asked the loudest, or who the requestor was. It seemed like no matter what task he chose, someone was unhappy.

Other times, he would rush and complete a request quickly for someone who had said it was urgent, only to go by that person's desk days later and see it still sitting there.

Then one day, he realized, "Maybe I should ask more questions. What's the worst they could say: 'I need it right now'?" He realized that, more often than not, he could negotiate a little extra time and put their requests into his plan, where it worked better for him. All he had to do was ask.

THE FIVE-PART MODEL TO INFLUENCE OTHERS

When you're making requests to others, you must tell them when you need it and why. You are actually helping others by giving them a deadline and reason so they can accurately prioritize your request. Be sure they understand by saying "yes"; be sure they understand that you're now depending on them to come through.

Ringmaster Tip: When you tell someone you need it ASAP, your request will probably go on the bottom of their list. Now they're the Ringmaster (because you've given them control over when they do it) and you're the Beast. Don't water down your deadline because you sympathize with how busy they are.

This is how the Ringmaster writes and speaks his requests:

1. *Could you please...?* (to induce cooperation using the right tone)
2. *Either way* (to get them to say yes, no, or at least something)
3. *Make your request specific* (to avoid questions)
4. *Give a specific deadline* (to help prioritize your request)
5. *Mention the consequences, good and bad* (if they don't meet your deadline)

By putting your request in the form of a question it tells the reader or listener that "Action is required." An open ended question softens the tone of a direct request. The words could and please are positive tone words to induce cooperation. Be sure you don't leave out Step 5. The number nine reason for procrastination is the other person doesn't see or hear why your request is so important. Step 5 will involve the other person in your deadline. If you don't include Step 5 then the deadline you give someone else will just be your deadline.

You have asked others to be more specific with you when they are making requests, and now you're going to be more specific in making requests of them. It's a win-win situation for both of you.

HOW TO NEGOTIATE REQUESTS

When the phone rings, the person on the other end usually tells you he needs something done immediately. It's urgent. The first question you need to instinctively ask yourself is, "Is it really?" This is a tough question.

I used to assume by the tone of a person's voice or his or her position in the company what the priority of the request was. Boy, did I get fooled a lot! The next time someone calls with a request, ask, "When is the latest I could get that to you?" You may be surprised at the answer. We assume the person needs it now, when perhaps the end of the day or tomorrow would be fine. You're trying to determine where that task falls in your matrix.

A CASE STUDY

When Jennifer looked at her list at the end of the day, the big tasks that she didn't really like to do were the only ones left on her list. She couldn't understand it. She always seemed busy all day long. She thought to herself, "I'm overworked." Then she kept track of her time for a week and discovered the following factors that were contributing to her dilemma.

When she got into work first thing in the morning, she worked on e-mail. Next thing she knew, it was time for a break. She started her day with the tasks that she enjoyed the most and that didn't take a lot of time. (She could get them off her list.) Every time she thought about starting that difficult task, she kept saying, "I don't have enough time now. I'll wait until 3 p.m. when I'll have more time." (Then, when it got toward the end of the day, she said, "Oh well, I'll start it tomorrow.")

She found that every time someone came by to ask for something, she dropped what she was doing without asking any questions. It seemed like she was jumping from task to task all day. She wondered, "Am I giving up what I'm currently working on without any fight?"

She started thinking, "Why am I doing what I'm doing, when I'm doing it?" She realized that she was shooting herself in the foot all day long. When she changed the way she handled her day, she actually started to go home on time.

SUCCESSFUL PEOPLE DO ONE THING AT A TIME

Most people try to do several things at once. Studies show successful people do only one thing at a time. They realize it will take them less time instead of jumping around. They are able to concentrate better, do the job in less time, and make fewer errors.

Consider what it's like when you're talking on the phone and trying to read and write e-mail. Both take longer, and the person on the phone can tell you're doing something else while you're talking to them. The ability to work on one thing at a time takes discipline. Aren't you kind of a traffic cop at work? Successful people either:

- Put off the interruption long enough to finish what they're working on. (This is the fastest way to improve the number of tasks you're completing daily and weekly.)

or

- Accept the interruption because it's a higher priority. When this happens, they make a note regarding important thoughts or ideas, and where they are with the task in the file and then put it back on their list.

SEE IF YOU CAN FIT IT INTO YOUR SCHEDULE

Successful people have learned to negotiate a way to fit the interruption or request into their Daily List. Can you create a win-win situation where you fit their request into your day when it fits more efficiently for you and still works for them?

This isn't the way I used to think. I used to jump every time I got a request. I realized that I needed to change my thought process. I needed to stop thinking, "Jump first," and instead start thinking, "Where can I fit their requests where it works better for me but still works for the requestor?"

Once I started to ask questions and batch my tasks more effectively, I started to negotiate requests so they fit better into my schedule. But remember: you need to have a Master List, or you will forget these requests and people won't let you work their requests into your schedule.

WRITE DOWN THE TASK AND CIRCLE THE DEADLINE

If you do successfully negotiate a better time to complete the task, be sure that you write down what you've agreed to on your Master List. Circle the deadline you've agreed to. Stick to your word. If you don't, you may lose your negotiating privileges with that person in the future.

TIP: If possible, deliver before the negotiated deadline and you'll look like a superstar!

SHOW YOUR LEADER AND TEAM MEMBERS YOUR PLAN

When your leader comes to you with something very important to him or her, show him your list. Show your leader what you're working on and what other tasks you have to complete that day. This is impossible to do if you didn't put your plan in writing the night before.

Ask your leader to prioritize your work according to when he really needs it by. It's faster and more accurate if he determines the priority. See if you can reschedule the other tasks you have, so that you can fit the new one in, or fit the request where it really belongs on your Master or Daily List.

TIP: It's in your best interests to educate your boss as to what you currently have on your plate, existing deadlines, and your ability to keep track of the huge workload you already have by using your Master List.

Your boss may see that you have a full plate of important tasks already and delegate the task to someone else. The same is true with team members. By showing them your list, they can see what you're working on and what is important to you.

A CASE STUDY

Gail was a hard worker. She always said yes. Her boss would come to her no matter how busy she appeared and say, "Could you get this done for me?" She felt like saying, "Sure—I can't get done what I currently have, but can I have another task?" It seemed like her boss had amnesia.

She thought, "Maybe I should show him my list and see what's important, or ask for clarification." The first time she asked this, her boss said, "I had no idea you were this busy. Keep working on what I've already given you, and I'll find someone else to complete this." She thought, "I wish I had said something sooner."

QUICK TIPS

✓ An A priority is a task or project with a specific deadline to be completed today and they've told you why their deadline is so important.

✓ A B priority is equally as important as an A priority but it doesn't have a specific deadline to be completed today.

✓ Work on your B priorities a little each day so they don't become A priorities. It's a lot less stressful.

✓ If someone says they need something ASAP, ask them when they specifically need it by, otherwise you don't accurately know whether it's an A or a B.

✓ The new prioritizing approach is:
- How much time do you have available?
- How much energy to you have at this moment?
- What is the best task you could pick based on the first two factors?

✓ Make sure you give others a deadline for finishing a task or responding, and the consequences, good or bad, for meeting or not meeting that deadline.

✓ Be sure to put your requests in the form of an open-ended question, using the right tone, to induce cooperation.

✓ Make sure human nature isn't affecting which task you choose.

✓ Successful people do one thing at a time.

✓ Don't give up working on your current task or project so easily.

✓ Try to defer the newest request until you finish what you're currently working on or at least get to a good spot where you could stop.

✓ If you have to stop working on your current task, make some notes or bullets so you know where you left off when you start again.

✓ See if you can negotiate requests where they work best for you but still work for the requestor.

✓ Be sure you write the task and specific deadline you've negotiated on your Master List so you won't forget to do it on time.

6

Controlling E-mail and Using Your E-mail System More Effectively

If you wish to succeed in managing and controlling others—
learn to manage and control yourself.

—WILLIAM J. H. BOETCKER

E-mail is the most abused form of communication in the workplace today. I believe it's the number one reason why communication in Corporate America has never been worse. That's why a number of companies are experimenting with outlawing e-mail once a week.

Many think that e-mail is the answer to everything, so the quality of our communication has really suffered. It is also one of the easiest ways to waste time under the disguise of doing something worthwhile.

To be effective, you need to really have discipline when it comes to e-mail. E-mail is a love/hate relationship: love to get it, hate what's in it. It's like an emotional roller coaster. I'm drained by the end of the day. In this chapter, we're going to look at

- How to control e-mail
- How to manage e-mail using the organizational tools in Outlook

HOW TO CONTROL YOUR E-MAIL

Here are some strategies I use to control e-mail so I can reduce the time I spend on receiving and sending e-mail every day.

Turn Off Your E-mail Notification and Check E-mail Periodically

E-mail is one of the biggest interruptions in today's workplace. If your machine automatically notifies you that you've just received an e-mail, turn that function off, especially in your veggie time. It is better to keep it turned off all day and set up times to check it or, alternatively, to leave it on all day and check it only once per hour.

I have trouble with discipline. If I left my e-mail open all day, I'd respond to it and interrupt myself every time I heard it go "ding." Human nature is "last in/first out." To counter this impulse, I trained myself to check my e-mail only once an hour (at the top of every hour) and as seldom as twice in the morning and twice in the afternoon, unless I'm expecting an important message. In that case, I turn on the visual notification to let me know a new message has arrived.

Worst case, turn off your e-mail notification and check it every 60 minutes. When you check your e-mail, you are the Ringmaster; when it goes "ding," you are the Beast.

TIP: Tell people that if they have a time-sensitive question or request that needs attention sooner than in one hour, they should call you instead.

In the worst case, turn on the visual notification so an envelope appears when a message arrives. That way, you know it's there and can finish what you're working on. To turn your audible and/or visual notification off, go to "Notification."

A CASE STUDY

E-mail was a big part of Ed's life. The first thing Ed did every day was check his e-mail. In fact, it got so bad that he started checking his e-mail from home before he even got to work that day. Next thing he knew, it was 10 a.m. and he hadn't started working on anything important yet.

Then, every time his computer went "ding," he would temporarily stop whatever he was doing and check it. Often, he would be disappointed at the message he would receive. (E-mail was a love/hate relationship.) It also seemed that when he was responding to e-mail, other people knew he was doing e-mail and would send more. (It was as if he opened e-mail and couldn't close it.)

He knew he had to do something. He had to become the Ringmaster and take control of e-mail. He realized that if he closed his e-mail and checked it periodically throughout the day, he would become the Ringmaster.

Once he turned off his e-mail and set up convenient times to check it every day, he got an hour more of work done every day.

If You Have to Check Your E-mail First Thing

First, change your screen view to Preview so you can see the subject line and the first three to four lines of the message. Go to

VIEW>AUTO PREVIEW. This feature will allow you to scan your e-mails faster and determine which ones you really need to respond to first thing in the morning. I don't have time to read the whole message to determine its priority. Delete any e-mails that are spam immediately so you have fewer.

TIP: In the first time slot each day, you're only looking for e-mail veggies that have a specific deadline to be done today and their importance is explained. If the e-mail isn't a veggie either put it on your master list and come back to it later or delete it.

You need to get your senders to put their purpose in the subject line and what they need you to do and the specific deadline in the first paragraph (discussed in Chapter 2). Then you can pick a few of the most important messages, respond to them, and close your e-mail.

Use the six tasks you wrote on your Daily List the night before as a filter to determine if an e-mail message is a veggie or not. If a message isn't a higher priority than what you already have on your list, pass on responding to it until the next time you're scheduled to check e-mail. That way, you can get started on a veggie faster and get out of e-mail.

Batch Your Responses to E-mail

When you are doing one thing at a time, it will take less time. By checking your e-mail at regular intervals (say, once an hour or four times a day), you can concentrate on handling only your e-mail and finish faster. This way you are really only doing one thing at a time, which will make responding to e-mail go much faster.

Give yourself 10 to 15 minutes to handle as many messages in your in-box as you can, in the correct priority (using the veggie principle), then close it and work on something else.

Rules for Using Instant Messenger

Most people that I encounter don't have enough discipline to use Instant Messenger. It can instantly ruin your productivity and reduce what you accomplish in a day. I still believe it's more effective to set up a telephone appointment or meeting than to go back and forth in Instant Messenger when you need to have a discussion or ask questions.

By leaving Instant Messenger open all day, you will set yourself up to jump from task to task, and the number of tasks or activities you complete in a day will suffer. We've already discussed how damaging interruptions can be: The decision is yours.

There is one exception to this rule. If Instant Messenger is set up ahead of time to assist in the completion of a project or task by making it easier to ask questions and have a real-time discussion (at a distance), this tool would be appropriate.

Only Handle E-Mail Once—Take Action

Act on and respond to your messages the first time that you read them. Go through and delete first, then act on the most important ones and, finally, file the rest so your in-box stays clean.

DON'T USE YOUR IN-BOX AS YOUR TO-DO LIST

The fastest way to fall behind and get in trouble is to use your in-box as your to-do list. It's the same as having piles on your desk. The rule is to never have more than one screen of e-mail messages in your in-box. The average person wastes 30 minutes a day looking for e-mail messages.

The first time you read a message, take one of the following actions immediately:

- Take action and then file it.
- Flag then file it for future action.
- Drag and drop it on your schedule or set a reminder for when you want to work on it.
- Delete it or read it and then delete it.

Just Say No

Tell people by phone or e-mail to take you off that mailing or CC list if you don't need to be on it. If you don't say something, it will keep coming.

TIP: Tell your direct reports which projects you want to be CC'd on; otherwise, they'll CC you on everything.

What to Do with Spam

Spam can come in many different forms. Delete them immediately and don't even open them. If you open them, it will tell the sender they've reached a "live" e-mail address.

Rules for Using E-mail Rather than the Phone

E-mail	Phone
Need only information	Need an immediate response
Provides a written backup	Need to ask questions
Some respond faster to e-mail	Want to hear someone's voice
Multiple people can receive it	Privacy

TIP: E-mail technically doesn't have any tone. It's whatever a person perceives you meant when they read your e-mail. If you're not sure how a person will interpret your e-mail message, call him or her instead, or call before you hit the Send key so they can hear your voice and understand the meaning of your e-mail.

E-mail often takes less time than telephoning and can be easier than taking notes, especially when you are busy. E-mail is for information; the telephone is for discussion. If you need a discussion, pick up the phone and call them.

Use Your Calendar to Show Your Schedule

Use your online calendar to show the meetings that you have scheduled, the appointments you've made, and the time you're blocking off to get important projects completed on time. That way, others will know when you're available and the best time to schedule a meeting.

USE YOUR E-MAIL SYSTEM TO MANAGE YOUR E-MAIL

Whether you use Lotus Notes, Outlook, or GroupWise, there are many tools you can use that will save you an amazing amount of time. The key is that each week you should learn how to use a different tool and actually implement it. In the near term you will have to spend additional time, but in the long term the leverage you create is well worth it.

These tools may be located in different places in Lotus Notes, Outlook, and GroupWise, but many easy to understand manuals are available that will explain exactly how to do these strategies. Here are some tools and strategies that are easy to set up that will make your work day much easier.

Turn Off Your E-mail Notification

When you check e-mail you are the Ringmaster. If your e-mail goes "ding" or you see the visual notification, you may interrupt yourself to check the message. TOOLS>OPTIONS>E-MAIL OPTIONS. Next, select ADVANCED E-MAIL OPTIONS.

Go to WHEN NEW ITEMS ARRIVE, and be sure the sound option isn't checked. If you have to know when e-mails arrive at least only have the envelope option on.

Be sure that the box that says, DISPLAY A NOTIFICATION MESSAGE WHEN NEW MAIL ARRIVES, isn't checked.

Use Auto Preview or the Preview Pane to Save Time Opening E-mail

Instead of having to open every e-mail message, use the Preview window or pane to save time. Teach your senders to let you know:

1. Why they're sending you an e-mail in the subject line

2. What they need and when they need it by in the first paragraph

Go to VIEW>AUTO PREVIEW. Another option under VIEW is to select READING PANE. Select either the bottom or to the right and you will see your folders, then in-box, then a specific message (if your reading pane is to the right).

Set Up Electronic Folders and Subfolders

If you have more than one screen of e-mail messages in your in-box you probably have a problem with your file system. If it takes too long to find a message, you will probably keep it in your in-box.

Try not to have too many main folders. Try to have no more than 10 main folders with subfolders under each mail folder.

TIP: The file names and categories you use in e-mail should be the same as the files and categories in your desk. Here are some examples of file names or headings:

- Action required (often your leader or customer)
- Clients and/or prospects
- Fingertip reference
- Meetings
- Delegate
- Projects (set up a separate folder for each project)

Color-Code Your Inbound E-mails

The fastest way to determine the importance of e-mail messages is to color-code them based on sender. This will make messages from your leader, team members, or clients stand out in your in-box when you receive them. That way when you open your e-mail you'll be drawn to those e-mails first.

Go to TOOLS>ORGANIZE>USING COLORS. Highlight a message in your in-box and the sender's name will automatically appear in the box that dropped down. Now select a color you want to use and hit APPLY COLOR. Now every past, present, and future message from that person will appear in that color.

Note: It isn't permanent. You can always change it back to black (the default color) or a different color by repeating the same steps described above.

Turn on the CC Filter If You Want to See Messages Only Sent to You

If you are on the CC line, that implies FYI (for your information). When you are on the TO line, that implies action required by you. By turning this feature on, it will make the messages that contain action required stand out. Go to TOOLS>ORGANIZE>USING COLORS and go to the second bullet down, "Messages sent only to me now appear in blue". Click TURN ON, and messages where you were on the TO line will appear in blue.

Flag Messages or Drag and Drop Them onto Your Calendar

The first time you see a message and it doesn't require immediate attention, flag it or drag and drop it onto your calendar so you set up time to
work on it and don't forget it. The flag feature is available by right-
clicking on a message and choosing the appropriate reminder. To the
far right side of each message is also a blank "flag" you can click on
and choose the appropriate flag based on the reminder you want to set.

Create Rules to Move and Block Certain E-mails

This is a wonderful feature that can help you manage your in-box.
This feature can eliminate unwanted e-mails and automatically
move certain e-mails right into the appropriate folder without clog-
ging up your in-box.

    You can set up a junk-mail filter that will automatically delete
messages based on the sender or the message. This is done by going
to TOOLS>ORGANIZE>USING FOLDERS. The shortcut is to
right-click on your mouse on CREATE RULE>FROM/OR BY
SUBJECT>MOVE THE ITEM TO>SELECT A FOLDER
(JUNK)>OK.

    The procedure is the same if you want messages from certain
people or departments to go to a preselected file folder without
directly going into your in-box. In the example above you would
select the appropriate file folder instead of the JUNK file folder. You
will see a number in blue next to that file folder when you receive a
message that you haven't read.

Clean Out Your Files Regularly by Archiving

Make time at the end of each day and the end of each week to go through and see if there are any files you don't need any more. A shortcut is to set up the AUTO-ARCHIVE option. Click on TOOLS>OTHER>AUTO-ARCHIVE, and check the appropriate boxes to whatever you're comfortable with. Each file can be set up to achieve different purposes.

Use the Mailbox Cleanup Feature

Go to TOOLS>MAILBOX CLEANUP>FIND ITEMS, and put 365 days. It will bring up any messages that are more than a year old. Ask yourself, "Do I still need these in my active files on in-box, or should I delete or archive them?"

As you get more organized you can adjust that to a shorter period of time so it will be easier to keep your files managed more effectively.

Set Up Spell Check

Most e-mail systems have a spell check feature. You have to set it up manually. In Outlook go to TOOLS>OPTIONS>SPELLING. Check the following boxes:

- Always check spelling before sending.
- Ignore original message text when replying or forwarding

- Always suggest replacement words for misspelled words.
- Use autocorrect when Word isn't the e-mail editor.

This will save you a lot of time proofing your e-mail. Remember, you still have to check your grammar.

Track Your Messages Using the Read Receipt Function

Go to TOOLS>OPTIONS>E-MAIL OPTIONS>TRACKING OPTIONS>READ RECEIPT and/or DELIVERY RECEIPT. This may warn you of a potential problem so you can follow up. You will receive a notification when your recipient opens your e-mail.

Note: This isn't always accurate because if your recipient uses AUTO PREVIEW, they may have seen and read your e-mail, but you won't get a notification.

Organize Your In-Box by Date, Sender, or Topic

When you open your in-box, go to TOOLS>ORGANIZE>USING VIEWS, to choose the way you want to handle your incoming messages. The short cut is to simply change the view on the line right under your INBOX heading. Your choices are by:

- Sender
- Date received
- Topic
- Follow-up flag

Create a Signature to Help Your Recipients

A simple signature at the end of your e-mails allows your recipients to see three alternative ways to reach you. They should be no longer then six lines.

Go to TOOLS>OPTIONS>SIGNATURES. Make sure it includes your:

- Name
- Company name
- Department and title
- Mailing address
- Phone number
- Fax number

Most signatures include the corporate Website address and some form of legal disclosure. Signatures should be no longer than six lines and *not* include a motivational quote from a dead person.

If You're Going to Be "Out of the Office"

Use your e-mail like you would your voice mail. If you're going to be out of the office, adjust your sender's expectation of a quick response by setting up the Out of Office feature. Try to offer them the option of contacting another person in your place and specify their e-mail address and/or phone number. This will tell your sender immediately that you're out of the office for a specific period, so they can contact someone else in your place until you return or wait until you return if they chose.

Go to TOOLS>OUT OF OFFICE ASSISTANT>I am cur-rently out of the office. In "AutoReply only once to each sender with the following text", type the message you want senders to receive while you're away and click OK. Be specific and not too long with your message.

QUICK TIPS

✓ Turn off your notification and check for messages periodi-cally. If you have to check e-mail first thing, use the Preview function and only look for veggies.

✓ If you have to check e-mail first thing in the morning, only look for veggies and come back to the other ones after you finish one of your veggies.

✓ Color-code incoming messages from your most important senders so that they'll stand out.

✓ Use the CC filter to see messages in blue when you were on the TO line. This denotes action required by you.

✓ Batch your responses to e-mail so they take less time.

✓ Don't use Instant Messenger unless you really need to.

✓ Use Auto Preview to see the subject line and the first three lines of each message. That way you don't have to open every message to see what it's about.

✓ Each time you check your e-mail, delete, take action, or put messages into folders and set up a reminder.

✓ Ask to be taken off mailing lists unless you really need to be "in the loop."

✓ Keep your in-box clean. Don't use it as your to-do list.

✓ Set up folders and subfolders that match the filing system in your desk.

✓ Create rules to move and delete certain incoming messages.

✓ Flag messages for further action.

✓ Set up spell check so every message is automatically checked before it's sent.

✓ Use the phone not e-mail when you need a discussion. E-mail is for information and the phone or a meeting is for discussion.

✓ When the content of your message is sensitive, call the person instead.

✓ Track your important, time-sensitive messages using the Read Receipt function

✓ Organize your in-box by date, sender, or topic using views to find messages.

✓ When you are trying to catch up on your filing, start with your most recent messages and work backwards toward the older messages in your in-box.

✓ Use the Out of Office feature when you're not going to be at work. Direct the sender to someone else who can help him or her in your absence.

✓ Use the calendar function to show others your schedule.

✓ Spend a little time each week getting to know a new feature of Outlook.

7

Organizing Your Writing and Speech to Get Faster Results

*If you wish to succeed in managing and controlling others—
learn to manage and control yourself.*

—WILLIAM J. H. BOETCKER

USE YOUR SUBJECT LINE TO GET YOUR READER TO OPEN YOUR E-MAIL

The fastest way to speed up responses to your e-mail messages is to improve your subject line. Use your subject line to tell the reader what your e-mail is about. Don't use it to announce the topic. Make them curious about your e-mail. Make your subject line stand out in his in-box. All readers want to know:

- Why did I get this e-mail?
- What do I have to do, if anything?
- When do you need it?

The average reader decides in 5 to 10 seconds whether to take action on your e-mail, file it, or delete it. To create more urgency, move the deadline into the subject line.

People often respond first to the ones that look easy or won't take a lot of time. A reader's first impression when he opens your message is the most important. If your e-mail message looks complicated and difficult to read and/or understand, he/she will often close or delete it.

A CASE STUDY

Bryan relied heavily on others for help and information when it came to the projects he was working on. His only problem was that everything seemed to take a long time. He would send a three-page e-mail and not get an answer for two weeks. He never stopped to realize that maybe he was part of the problem. However, he did realize that without timely responses from coworkers, he would never be able to leave work on time.

He asked a friend to look at some messages he was having trouble getting answers to. He asked her if she could tell him what she thought the problem was. "It's easy. I wouldn't respond either."

"But why?" he asked.

She said, "If I can't tell what an e-mail message is about quickly and you're not my boss, I'll either delete it or try to come back to it later. When I open your e-mail, I can tell it's going to take a while to read, so I try to come back to it later when I have more time."

She continued, "You also need to provide a deadline and a reason why a timely response is so important. When you write 'ASAP,' it doesn't really motivate me to respond quickly." When Bryan started to write for the reader using deadlines, he started to receive answers much sooner.

WHAT IS THE PURPOSE OF YOUR LETTER OR E-MAIL?

Before you begin typing, you need to define the purpose of your message. Many writers find that their letter or e-mail misses the point because their message fails to identify this first. Because many writers begin with background information, they don't really see the purpose until they finish writing the letter or e-mail. Also, they come up with a subject line that's very general.

Are you trying to persuade, inform, ask/respond to a question, or thank someone? After you decide and write down your purpose, you're ready to consider your audience. What kind of style will they respond to?

HAVE ONE KEY POINT OR ISSUE PER MESSAGE

The rule in e-mail is one subject or issue per e-mail. If you have multiple issues, action items, or requests, tell the reader in the first paragraph so he will know. If you don't, they will probably only respond to one question or request and you will need to resend the e-mail or make a new request.

Now add white space and make your request or ask your questions using bullets or numbers.

CONSIDER YOUR READER OR AUDIENCE BEFORE YOU WRITE

One of the biggest mistakes that most writers make is that they don't take time to consider the reader before they begin writing. The more you know about your audience, the more you can customize your letter or e-mail. See if you can visualize your reader as you get to know your reader:

- Who is your reader?
- How much does the reader know about your subject? (This will determine how much information or background you'll need to include.)
- Are they young or old, male or female?
- What do they respond best to? Do they like short, to-the-point messages or messages that start out with some small talk?

UNDERSTAND YOUR OVERWHELMED READER

Your readers may be getting many types of interruptions from many different sources. Let's look at some of the other tasks distracting your audience:

- Responding to other e-mail messages
- Trying to finish a task or project with a nearing deadline

- Handling interruptions from coworkers or noise
- Answering the telephone or cell phone
- Preparing for a meeting
- Relationship building with other employees or peers

Ask yourself, "what's going to make them read my e-mail message instead of doing all of those other things?" Is your message well written enough to get them to open it the moment Outlook goes "ding"?

YOUR MESSAGE SHOULD HAVE THESE THREE CHARACTERISTICS

It should be:

1. Short
2. To the point
3. Easy to read and understand, with retention

UNDERSTANDING WHAT'S AT STAKE

The average reader will decide within 5 to 10 seconds after they open your letter or e-mail whether to:

1. Read it and take action.
2. Put it into a file or pile of other papers and try to come back to it later, if they can find it.
3. Delete it or throw it away.

MAKE YOUR WRITING READER FRIENDLY

1. Use short, simple words (they're faster to write and easier for the reader to read).

2. Always try to finish your message with a deadline for the reader and a reason why they need to respond by your deadline.

3. Write in a bulleted, not paragraph, format when possible.

4. Make your e-mail look easy to read.

5. Keep your paragraphs short (no more than three to four lines in length).

6. Keep your sentences short so they're easy to read and understand. Make sure your sentences are less than 17 words long.

7. Keep the tone of your message positive. Check it before you send it.

USE THE PADD MODEL TO ORGANIZE YOUR WRITING

In order to make your e-mail easier and faster to write and easier and faster for your reader to read it, try this simple model next time you write.

PADD stands for:

- *Purpose:* Why you're sending this e-mail to the other person. (This goes in the subject line using four to eight words). Pretend it's a headline from a newspaper.

- *Action:* This is what you want the reader to do. (This goes in the first paragraph by itself so the action you want stands out to the reader.) Make sure you keep your first paragraph short, no more than two to three lines long.
- *Detail:* This is your bulleted or numbered list. (If you are writing in paragraph style, this is the body of your e-mail or the middle.)
- *Deadline:* Always try to finish your e-mail with a specific deadline and a logical reason for the deadline. (This will involve the reader in your deadline.)

Note: To add importance to your e-mail, include a specific deadline in the subject line instead of ASAP. The number one way to prioritize is based on a specific deadline.

An example of how to end your e-mail: Could you please get me these answers by 5 pm today otherwise I won't be able to finish this project today? (Don't say, "Thank you in advance." It really doesn't mean anything to the reader.)

IF YOU MUST FORWARD A MESSAGE, GIVE INSTRUCTIONS

Put your comments at the top in the subject line or first paragraph. This will save the reader time. "FYI" doesn't really tell the reader anything. A brief comment will take less than 30 seconds and could save each reader hours.

WHEN YOU HIT THE REPLY KEY, MODIFY THE SUBJECT LINE

Many people think it saves time to just hit the Reply key, type a message or response, and then hit the Send key. Pretty soon there is a long string of messages that each person has to read to follow the "e-mail trail." Try modifying the subject line with:

- My answer to... .
- My response to... .
- Your request or... .

This modification will show the reader that this is the most recent e-mail and its purpose quickly.

E-MAIL ETIQUETTE

Here are a few simple rules to ensure that you don't get in trouble and that get you the results you intended:

1. Your e-mail message is a reflection of you.
2. Your e-mail message is a reflection of your company.
3. Write your e-mail like it is a letter or memo. Don't use shortcuts or symbols.
4. Always reread your e-mail before you hit the Send key.
5. If the president of your company received your e-mail, what would he or she think?
6. Only mark your e-mail as urgent when it really is urgent.

7. E-mail is admissible in a court of law, so pick up the phone if it's sensitive.

8. Don't write anything you wouldn't say to someone in person.

9. Use simple formats, and stay away from fancy backgrounds.

10. How well you know the reader and/or the subject should dictate your level of formality and language.

QUICK TIPS

✓ Use your subject line to get your reader to open your e-mail message. Make it like a headline from a newspaper. Make your reader curious.

✓ Make your subject line six words long to make it detailed.

✓ Define the purpose of your e-mail before you begin writing.

✓ Have one key point or issue per message. If you are going to be discussing or asking for more than one thing, tell your reader in the first paragraph or they might miss it.

✓ Understand your overwhelmed reader. What's going to make them open your message and take action? Make your message short and easy to read and understand.

✓ Make your message:
  • Short and concise
  • To the point
  • Easy to read and comprehend

✓ The average reader decides in 5 to 10 seconds whether they are going to:

- Read your message and take action.
- Read part of your message and try to come back to it at a later time.
- Delete it.

✓ Be sure you use a cooperative tone when writing otherwise they might not respond to your message or take it the wrong way.

✓ Use the PADD model to organize your writing:

- Purpose
- Action
- Detail
- Deadline/why

✓ Keep your first paragraph short, no more than two to three lines long.

✓ Write using bullets or numbers instead of long paragraphs.

✓ Keep your sentences and paragraphs short so they're easy to read and understand.

✓ Always proof your writing before you hit the Send key.

✓ Use proper etiquette when sending messages.

✓ Don't use all CAPS; bold key points instead.

8

Organizing and Streamlining Your Projects

If you don't know where you're going, you'll end up
somewhere else.

—YOGI BERRA

We spend eighty percent of our time each day putting out fires. Successful completion of projects by the given deadline is what improves your company and gets you noticed. Projects seem to take forever to get started, so they are easy to procrastinate. The more difficult the project, the more tasks a project involves, the higher the probability you won't start it until the last minute, using a wing-it planning strategy. It doesn't have to be that way.

Remember, if planning and organizing take too long, human nature will prompt you to create short cuts, like winging-it. The key to project management is to learn to create a simple plan that is realistic (based on a typical day/week and past experience), and to create or block out the time when you are at your best mentally, to work on it.

The number one reason why projects either fail or are not completed on time is that they aren't set up correctly in the beginning. Organizing or setting up your project correctly is a thought process. When you follow the steps I have outlined in this chapter, in the order I have given you, you will consistently complete your projects on time or early and improve the quality of your work. Let's look at a new streamlined approach for getting your projects set up and completed on time.

WHAT IS THE OBJECTIVE OF YOUR PROJECT?

An objective is the end result that you direct your time, energy, and resources toward achieving both individually and as a team. It should define the outcome you desire and your purpose.

People are always asking for focus and concentration. In this world of distractions, those who can see the big picture and the end result have learned to "sprinkle" the fires around the tasks and projects that "drive" their company.

The reason this chapter is in the first half of the book is because organizing is a thought process. Improvement in organizational skills starts with improving your thought process so you think this way instinctively when you organize your projects, tasks that need to be completed, and your daily/weekly plan.

LEAVE ROOM IN YOUR PLAN FOR THINGS TO GO WRONG

The number one reason why people don't meet deadlines on time is because they didn't leave room for anything to go wrong. This is a key skill in organization. You must leave room for the unexpected or interruptions, in other words, for reality. Obstacles can be tangible or only in one's mind. This becomes a three-step process:

1. In the past, what happened to throw off your projected time line for finishing your project on time?

2. What is a "typical" chaotic day look like for you? Have you left room for interruptions, e-mail, phone calls, and assisting others?

3. What "unexpected" obstacles have come up in the past that you didn't anticipate or leave room for in your plan?

Again, you should have a contingency plan in place before you start. Sometimes when we plan our project, we act like nothing has ever gone wrong in the past. By anticipating potential obstacles, you'll also have less stress and feel more in control when they do come up. When you leave room in your plan for things to go wrong, you have more confidence you're going to meet your deadline.

TIP: The past is an excellent indicator of the future. If you carefully examine the past, you will see the typical obstacles that have surfaced and will be able to leave room for them next time.

Yet, rather than learning from the past, many people set up their projects the same way, only to fail again. For some reason, something in their minds said, "This time it's going to be different! I feel really good it's all going to work out this time." This time, try to take a "worst case" scenario when planning and, if fewer things go wrong, you might actually finish early.

You may often be given projects and be forced to make assumptions in the beginning. If you make assumptions, be sure that you share them with your boss or whoever gave you the project. Ask as many questions as you can in the beginning to get a good understanding of the desired end result. At the end of each week, review your assumptions and be prepared to make changes.

I see people all the time who start their goal or project based on assumptions, some of which prove correct while others don't. They get to the end of the first week and they don't hit their target for that week, so they say, "See, this project deadline isn't realistic!" Don't give up. Add your new information and reset your plan.

TIP: It is better to underpromise and overdeliver than to overpromise and underdeliver.

FOCUS ON YOUR PROJECT AND WORK ON IT WHEN YOU'RE AT YOUR BEST

These days, we are so focused on putting out the fires that progress toward finishing our projects on time is very slow or nonexistent. Eighty percent of your evaluation is based on the number of projects you complete and the quality of your execution. Only 20 percent of your evaluation is based on how many fires you put out daily and annually.

Yet we spend 80 percent of each day putting out fires and 20 percent of each day working on what really matters most, both to you and to the company.

If your activity doesn't contribute directly toward completing your project, you may be wasting your time. Without honesty, you may not be able to see that you're working on the wrong thing at the wrong time. Remember: putting out fires is a maintenance issue. Putting out fires just helps maintain the status quo. If you solve the cause of the fire and fix it, that's something that improves the company and will get you noticed.

Projects are top priorities for most major companies and must receive that placement when you're considering your daily, weekly, monthly, and quarterly plan. You must put your project plan into your calendar first, because these projects are the highest priority. Otherwise, your daily, weekly, and monthly plans won't be as effective as they could be.

A CASE STUDY

Pauline was a hard worker. She was always helping others and other divisions with questions and putting out fires. One day, her boss came to her desk. He asked, "What have you been working on lately?" She said, "I have really been helping other divisions put out fires." He replied, "What progress have you made on the projects I've given you?"

She replied, "I haven't had a chance to start them yet." Her boss then made it clear that if something didn't change, she wouldn't be there to put out any more fires. (Do you get my meaning?) When Pauline changed her thinking, she realized how much easier it was to prioritize and how much better she felt about what she got done.

TIP: People are seldom recognized and promoted for putting out fires. People are rewarded for solving the cause of the fire, making the company money, or saving the company money.

As I mentioned earlier, what you want to do is to be sure that you work every day on tasks that apply to your projects and that you sprinkle out the fires around them. The trick is that your projects have to go into your plan first, not last, and not at the end of the day. Otherwise, you'll try to put them off until tomorrow, and tomorrow ends up being very close to your deadline.

TO ACCURATELY SET UP YOUR PROJECT, IT'S IMPORTANT THAT YOU...

- Have a clear vision of what the expected deliverable is at the end of your project before you begin. The Ringmaster continues to ask questions until he or she is crystal clear on the requestor's desired outcome. It's faster to ask questions and be 100 percent right than to start with little or no information and have to do it all over again. This will also have you prioritize your work more accurately.

- Make sure your requestor has a clear vision of what they expect the end result of the project to be. Because everyone is moving so quickly, often requestors will be vague when they assign tasks and/or projects. This can set you up for failure or delivering the wrong end result. The more questions you ask the requestor, the clearer the desired end result will become to the requestor. That way, both of you will be on the same page with little room for misunderstanding.

- Make sure that you check with your resources or other groups that you're going to need help from to get their commitment or buy-in before you begin your project. Make sure they are an available resource. This will also help them plan ahead. If you don't, how can you be sure your deadline is realistic and achievable?

NINE EASY STEPS TO EFFECTIVE PROJECT MANAGEMENT

1. See the End Result in Your Mind

Close your eyes and picture what your project will look like when you reach the end result. Now work backward and write as you go. A major problem is that people tend to leave out obvious steps when they are putting their project together. You will reduce the chance that you'll make this mistake if you really see it in your mind.

Now clearly define what the end result of your project will look like in a specific statement. Check with your requestor before you begin to make sure that statement is the deliverable he is expecting. The more clearly defined your end result is, the greater the chance you will achieve it accurately and by the deadline.

2. Write Down a Start and Completion Date

Writing down a specific start and completion date will increase your focus and the likelihood of completing your project on time. If you don't do this, chances are you will continue to put off working on your project until it becomes urgent.

If you didn't get a start and/or end date when you got that project, ask for one. If you still can't get one, make one up and tell your boss. Now you have to start. How many times have you been given a task or project without a deadline, when all of a sudden you get a call and the task or project is now urgent? Don't let it happen to you!

3. Break Down Your Project by Brainstorming

Begin by brainstorming. See the desired end result in your mind, and then start writing down the steps, the tasks, and ideas as they come to mind. Just make notes, whatever pops into your head first, in no particular order. Most people don't realize that is easier and faster for your mind to organize a project if it can *see* all of the steps or tasks that you need to complete. It is much slower and less accurate for the mind to recall all of the necessary steps/tasks to be completed in the right order.

Remember: planning and organizing are a task and a checkmark. This will get you going.

Make sure that you write down as much as you can about your project. There is a direct correlation between the amount of writing you do on your project or task and the probability of success. The more you write down, the higher the probability you're going to succeed. The more you write down, the larger the commitment you're making to complete your task or project.

It's like when a computer downloads a picture. When it first appears, it's very fuzzy. As it continues to download, the picture becomes more and more focused until the picture is crystal clear. It's the same concept here. Remember, your mind is very visual. When it sees that you've put a lot down in writing, it sends the message, "We might as well do it; you've already spent all this time writing about it!"

The number one reason for procrastination is that the project or task seems too large or difficult. How many times have you put off something and had to allocate one whole day to get it done? Here are some ways to avoid putting off working on your project:

- Break your project down into 22 workdays a month so you can work on it a little each day and it won't seem so difficult or unpleasant. That way, if you get derailed for one day, it won't be a big deal. You won't feel the same stress because you still have plenty of time to work on it.
- Start your project as close as you can to the day you receive it. Don't wait until you're up against the deadline. The day you get the project, start brainstorming. By brainstorming, you're actually moving forward. Just work on it a little every day instead of having to block out a whole day at the end. You'll have a lot less stress.

As I said, the number one reason why people put off tasks and projects is that they seem too involved and too difficult. Remember, though, that it's better to underpromise and overdeliver than to overpromise and never start. Just tell yourself, "I'm only going to work on this for 15 to 30 minutes. I'm going to see what I'm going to need to do and how I'm going to break the task into smaller parts." (In today's environment, is it very realistic to think you can block off large blocks of time when you usually have a lot of interruptions?)

In the prioritization section, you'll see that we often pick the task that's easiest or that doesn't take a lot of time to complete. When you break that task or project into smaller parts, it will compete with the smaller task you usually pick first. Next time you can't get started, say, "I'm just going to work on this for 15 minutes."

The more you break down your project, the more writing you'll do. When you finish writing, you'll probably say, "Hey, I could probably do this now!"

A CASE STUDY

A vice president of a local bank was very distressed. Her husband had a small business and had filed a tax extension. The extension would be over in four days. She had stressed about it all summer. She didn't see how she could get it filed in time. She couldn't even get started.

I told her to go home and work on it for about 15 to 20 minutes. Just do a couple of tasks. See if she could break the tax return into four parts and work on it a little each day. She agreed, and we parted ways.

Three days later, I went to see her and find out how she was doing. She said, "I can't believe it myself, but I mailed it in this morning, one day early." I asked her how she did it. She said that when she went home Monday night, she was very tired. It was 8 p.m., and she had just come from a Chamber of Commerce meeting. Even though she was tired, she remembered what I said and thought, "What the heck, I can work on it for 15 minutes."

She said, "I went upstairs and finished one task and thought that didn't take very long, so I did another and another. I realized this isn't such a big deal. I can probably do this. I then broke it down into two more days so I could finish early, and sure enough I did." Has this ever happened to you?

4. Identify Who You Are Going to Need

Be sure you write down in your plan who you're going to need help from and when before you begin.

TIP: Check with coworkers to see if they have the time to help and if your expectations and assumptions are correct before you begin.

A CASE STUDY

One time I bet my friends I could lose 20 pounds in 30 days. They all said, "How much do you want to bet? We'll even give you odds!"

At the end of 30 days, they were all waiting by my desk when I came into work. They asked, "Did you go on a reverse diet?" They were right: I had actually gained weight. Here's what I learned: I told my boss that I was starting a project and asked if I could meet with him in a week to make sure I was doing it correctly. Then I had to start it; I knew he would respond just as my friends had if I failed again.

---

5. Make Sure Your Deadline Is Realistic and Achievable

If you don't believe you can make your deadline, there is a high statistical probability you won't. In order to complete a project or task on time, it's important that you believe you can do it.

Here are the steps to make sure you believe you can deliver by the deadline:

- First break your project down by writing down into as many tasks and action items as you can. Then assign a timeframe for completing each step. Consider the past and how long something similar took to complete.

- If you don't believe the deadline is realistic and achievable, be sure you say something and explain why. Be sure you have a "solution" ready with some options for your boss to choose from.

TIP: No one likes a complainer. If you don't believe the goal is realistic, have a solution before you go to your boss. Become a "solution provider."

6. Identify What Could Go Wrong

Before you start, be sure you have a plan B. Based on past experience, what went wrong? Have you done a similar task in the past? What happened? The past is a great indicator of the future. Don't quickly dismiss things that have gone wrong in the past. It's like Murphy's law: if you don't leave room for things to go wrong, things will go wrong. How many times has that happened to you?

What's the worst that could happen if nothing goes wrong? You might finish early? Wouldn't that be a refreshing change?

7. Identify When You Are Going to Work on Your Project, Daily and/or Weekly

Ask yourself, "When, during the course of each day or week, am I going to work on my part of my project? What is the best block of time to reserve so I can spend quality time working on my project? Can I start it first thing in the morning so that I can get it out of the way and it isn't left on my list at the end of the day?" When you consider a "typical day" when are interruptions less than other times?

This is a more important step than you think. By doing this, you'll increase the chance of success. First, you'll be putting your project into your schedule at a specific time, so that you don't put it off to the end of the day; second, you'll be making a commitment; and third, you'll be using clear thought to pick the correct time to work on it.

8. Make Your Weekly/Monthly Results Measurable

When you set up your project, identify a goal for what you need to accomplish each week. That way each Friday afternoon you can measure whether you are on schedule or need to make adjustments next week. I see more people give up because they didn't get to where they wanted to be by the end of the first week. Remember, though, when you first set up the project, you were making assumptions based on limited information.

Cure: Stay flexible and anticipate that you're going to have to make adjustments at the end of each week so you won't get so discouraged. That's why you have to build extra time into your plan.

9. Write Down a Reward for Finishing on Time

Start rewarding yourself by simply writing down the history of your successes. As you complete each task, put a checkmark next to it or cross it off. Visual proof of completing tasks makes you feel successful. When you don't write down all the steps, you're not getting all the credit you deserve. The more you write down, the more you will complete, and the more checkmarks you will receive. Don't you want to get the credit you deserve?

Then, when you complete the task or project as a whole, provide yourself an even more tangible reward. It doesn't have to be a big deal. It's part of being good to oneself. The more difficult or unpleasant the task, the bigger you should make the reward. A reward shouldn't always be "a job well done."

Be sure you don't pick a reward that you do all the time anyway. That doesn't really mean anything. Pick a reward that will enhance your personal life. Your reward should be something you can picture in your mind doing, so that when the going gets tough, you can close your eyes and see yourself enjoying your reward. It's like putting the carrot in front of you.

Few of us may want to admit this, but isn't there something inside of us saying, "What's in it for me?" Make your tasks and projects more fun by motivating yourself to complete them.

Most people don't reward themselves after they complete a difficult task or project. They think that it's just part of their job. They think a reward is a "job well done." Rewarding yourself is part of being good to you. Some people wait until after they complete a task or project to reward themselves. There's no motivation in that. Some examples would be:

- When I get this done by noon, I'm going out to lunch.
- When I get this done by Friday at noon, I'm going to take a half-day and spend it with the kids.

- When I get this done this week, I'm taking my (wife or husband) out to that fancy restaurant and a movie.

QUICK TIPS

✓ A goal of a project is the end result that you direct your time, energy, and resources toward achieving both individually and as a team.

✓ Leave room for things to go wrong, for the unplanned, and for interruptions. Use what's happened in the past to guide your future planning.

✓ It's better to underpromise and overdeliver than to overpromise and underdeliver. Don't let the fires overwhelm your key projects and what matters most.

✓ Focus on your project when you are your best (the highest energy).

✓ Have a clear vision of what the expected deliverable is at the end of your project.

✓ Make sure your requestors have a clear vision of what they want. Don't be afraid to ask questions if their request is vague.

✓ Identify who you're going to need to help you with your project before you start, and be sure they can help. See the end result of your project in your mind before you start and clearly define it. After you see the end result, start brainstorming.

✓ Write down tasks and ideas as they pop into your head in no particular order. Start working on your project as soon as you get it.

✓ Write down a start and end date.

✓ Make sure the deadline is realistic and achievable. If it isn't, offer a solution.

✓ Identify when you're going to work on it each day and block out time on Outlook so you actually work on it.

✓ Make your weekly results measurable so you can make the needed adjustments to finish on time.

✓ Before you begin, write down a reward for finishing on time. Don't be afraid to give yourself mini-rewards along the way if it's a long-term project.

9

Effective Delegation That Works

---

*There is a great man who makes every man feel small. But the
really great man makes every man feel great.*

—CHINESE PROVERB

The most sought after management skill today is the ability to train
others. It sounds so easy. So why is it so difficult and why do so few
supervisors, managers, and leaders spend time cultivating and devel-
oping their direct reports? Training is an essential part of delegating
successfully. Companies are constantly asking their leaders to mentor, coach, and train their direct reports. The most common response
I hear is, "When do you think I have the time to do that? I barely
have enough time to get my own work done."

The problem with delegation and training is that it takes time
to save time. The average person says, "In the time it takes me to
train a direct report to do this task or project, I could have completed it myself." We take such a short term perspective. Delegation
requires a long-term perspective. One of the most important leadership skills today is to develop your direct reports. People always
want to be learning new things each day, to feel a part of. Help them

take ownership of their job and become successful at doing it and you will develop a loyal direct report.

One day my boss said to me, "Would you be willing to take the time to train your direct report to do that task correctly for the next 30 days, if I said you wouldn't have to do that task again for the next 11 months?" The first time I heard that I asked, "What do you call that?" Delegation my boss answered. He said, "You know I can't promote you until one of your direct reports can do your job well." I immediately got up and started walking out of his office. He asked me, "Where are you going?" I responded, "I going to back to my group and do some training."

Delegation is the act of passing responsibility for the completion of a task to another person. Delegation seems so easy, and you've been told it's one of the most effective time management tools available; yet, why does it rarely work, you wonder? From my discussions with managers at Hertz rental car locations in 1996, it was the number one reason they were burning out. Delegation wasn't working well in many instances, but they couldn't understand why.

Early in my career, I didn't understand the importance of delegation. As a result, I worked longer hours than I needed to and my staff depended heavily on me for everything (because I did all the thinking). It took me a long time to understand that I was only as strong a manager as the weakest person on my team. My father said to me one day, just before he retired, "I don't know why I come to work anymore; everyone knows my job." To me, that sums it all up.

Through research and trial and error, I have developed some foolproof steps that, if carefully followed, make it difficult to fail at delegation. Remember, the number one most desirable skill in managers today is the ability to train others well.

In this chapter, we're going to examine:

1. Why we don't delegate more
2. The benefits of successful delegation
3. What tasks to and not to delegate
4. The 10 easy steps to successfully delegate

WHY DON'T WE DELEGATE MORE? (THE OBSTACLES)

- We think we can do it faster and better than someone else can.
- It takes too much time and effort.
- We fear mistakes that we'll have to correct.
- We fear losing control; we don't want to let go.
- We lack faith in others (insecurity).
- It's outside our "comfort" zone.
- There is no one to delegate to.

Obstacles for Subordinates

- Lack of ability to do the selected task
- Lack of desire or interest in the task or project
- Inability to see why the task is so important
- Lack of enough information or specific expectations
- Lack of authority

BENEFITS OF SUCCESSFUL DELEGATION

1. It will save you an amazing amount of time by using your subordinates' time more effectively.

2. It's one of the highest forms of motivation known because it encourages participation or being a part of the group or plan.

3. It develops your staff into a more productive group.

4. It encourages trust and cooperation on your team.

5. It increases the level of teamwork for your subordinates.

6. It saves your company money by having the right person doing the job.

7. It allows you to improve your communication skills.

8. It will increase your self-confidence and abilities to manage others.

9. It will improve your teaching and coaching skills.

A CASE STUDY

Nathan was looking for an assistant. He asked his best friend if he knew anyone who would be interested. His friend told him his girlfriend was looking for a job and asked if he would talk to her. He said sure.

The next day they met, and the first thing he asked her was what her current salary was. (He did this to confirm what he had already heard.) When she said $50,000, he told her the job only paid $25,000 so she probably wouldn't be interested.

She then asked him for a job description. He told her that every day would be different, that she would have multiple job responsibilities, and that she would always be learning new things. She asked if she could think about it. Nathan was skeptical. Why would she want to take a 50 percent pay cut to come to work for him? He said fine.

The next day, she called him and said that she would like to take the job. Nathan asked why. She said, "Well, I do make twice as much at my current job, but I feel like I'm nothing more than a glorified gopher. With your job, I'd be constantly learning new things and have responsibility."

Unfortunately, after six months his new assistant quit for another job making $75,000 a year. She told Nathan the reason they hired her was because of all the things she learned while working for him.

USE YOUR MASTER LIST TO TRACK TASKS YOU'VE DELEGATED

Many managers and leaders know how to delegate tasks and projects but not how to keep track of what they've delegated and to whom. When delegating, the most important thing to remember is to put it in writing. This eliminates misunderstanding, improves communication, helps you track the task you delegated, and improves the chances the task will be done correctly and on time. If you delegate a lot, keep a notebook. Managers are delegating so quickly now that they can barely remember who they gave the task to.

Early in my career, I had a boss who never wrote anything down. He would delegate tasks to me, and I (knowing he didn't write it down) would wait to start on the project until he asked a second time. He would say the second time, "Didn't I ask you to work on the XYZ report?" I would say, "No, but I'd be happy to start it right away." After a while he learned; he started writing down the tasks he was delegating, and my loophole was gone.

This is what you'll need to write down:

1. The date you assigned the task
2. Who you assigned it to
3. A clear description of the task and your expectations
4. A review and due date
5. Notes from your discussion

THE 10 STEPS TO DELEGATING SUCCESSFULLY

1. Identify Tasks You Can Delegate

Write down all of the tasks or projects that you're responsible for or that you work on daily, weekly, and/or monthly. Using the criteria below, which tasks or projects could you delegate to your subordinates?

Remember, not everything you do can be delegated. Also, not that you'll run out and do this, but don't try to delegate everything at once. Develop a plan and timetable for delegating tasks you've identified as ones you can delegate. Discuss these tasks or projects with your subordinates, and check for interest level. Sometimes you may be very surprised at who's interested in doing what.

What to Delegate

- Tasks or projects that will benefit the company or division (tasks that mean something)

- Tasks or projects that will improve your abilities or performance
- Tasks or projects that will benefit subordinates' knowledge and confidence

What Not to Delegate

- Poorly defined tasks or projects where there's a high risk of failure
- Tasks or projects that require management involvement or decision-making authority

If Possible, Delegate the Whole Task

This will help designees develop the confidence to do the job on their own. Be supportive. This will increase their experience and sense of accomplishment. They will feel like they're a more important part of the team.

I used to see managers all the time have a direct report do most of the work on a project yet claim all the glory. If a direct report is already doing most of the work on a project, let him or her complete it and share the limelight.

Accept That Others Can Do the Project as Well

There are many ways to accomplish a task. Who knows—you may learn a new, more efficient way. It's been known to happen.

Early in my career, this was initially difficult for me to accept. When you're a young "hotshot," it's hard to believe someone else can do a task better than you. As I got older and was "forced" because of lack of time to delegate more tasks, I was constantly embarrassed to find out that my direct reports could do certain tasks as well as or better than I could. When I finally matured, I enjoyed watching my direct reports' successes, and I believe that's when I really became a good manager.

2. Choose the Right Person for the Job

- One of the easiest ways to determine the right person to work on a task or project is to ask your direct reports if anyone has an interest. This eliminates guessing, and a high percentage of the time he or she really is the right person.

- If you choose the person, tell your designee why you have chosen him or her for the task. (Make sure the person has adequate skills, knowledge, and interest to do the job.) A common question I hear all the time is, "How do you delegate so it doesn't seem like you're 'dumping'?" This tip will usually eliminate the feeling of being dumped on.

- Be sensitive to their feelings. Show your appreciation, especially when you're "dumping" a task on them.

- Adjust your expectations to the person's abilities.

- Ask the person to work on it as well as he can. You're available only if he gets completely stuck. Learning by one's mistakes can be very effective.

- If the person has a question, make him write it down before coming to you. It will make him more focused. It will also save you time and improve the person's retention.

- Ask the person to batch his questions so you can answer them all at once.
- Try starting with smaller tasks and build up, increasing the person's confidence.

A CASE STUDY

Gloria felt like every time she delegated a task or project to one of her direct reports, they seemed to resent her. She couldn't understand why. She also had difficulty getting them to complete it on time. The tasks and projects were coming so fast that she didn't have time to even think about who she was going to assign them to and why.

One day, she asked one of her direct reports how he felt when she delegated tasks to him. He said that the way she gave tasks to him made him feel like he was the "only person breathing in the area," so he got the task. Also, it was usually a task he thought she didn't want to do, so he got it. He didn't feel like she really had confidence in him. He wanted to feel like he was part of the team, constantly growing and learning new things.

From that day on, Gloria decided to spend more time when she delegated. She decided to first ask her direct reports for their interest level in different projects and tasks, to explain the importance of the task or project, and, when appropriate, why they were chosen to the task or project. The results were immediate. In addition, she also made the commitment to explain her expectations, to train her direct reports more thoroughly, and to improve her communication skills. Now they have a real team.

3. Define the Project, Desired Results, and Expectations

Be sure to set aside uninterrupted time with the person you delegate to so you can explain the task and make sure he knows what's expected. Don't assume that he knows how to do something. Don't end the meeting without full agreement that he completely understands all aspects of the task. Make the task seem important, or it may get put off.

If you are being delegated to and the desired results are vague, start asking questions until you can get a good feel for what your leader wants. Otherwise, chances are that you'll have to do it over again.

TIP: Give your direct reports an example of how you do the task, report, or project so they can follow the same format.

4. Establish a Starting and Ending Time

Make sure you are very specific about when you want your subordinates to start, when you'll be reviewing their progress, and the deadline for the task or project. Get them to put it on their calendar right away. You will write the task and designee in your logbook, along with a follow-up date on your Master List.

TIP: When delegating tasks, give employees sufficient time to schedule, set goals, and include the new assignment in their daily plan.

5. Agree on a Review Time and Don't Hover

If you delegate a task on Monday and it's due on Friday, set up a review time on Wednesday. (The review time should be halfway between the start and end date.) This will give you time to make adjustments, let them work on it alone, ensure the task is a success, and increase their confidence.

A CASE STUDY

Craig always wanted to have his hand in everything his direct reports did. He would call them daily and ask them if they were done yet. Talk about micromanaging. He couldn't understand why they seemed so agitated when he called for a "progress" report. He finally asked another manager if he had ever experienced the same thing.

His friend told him about a lesson that he learned the hard way: "I learned that for my people to grow, I have to give them the room to make mistakes and learn. When I gave them the room, often they would come up with a new way to do something that was much better than the way they used to do it. By reviewing progress halfway through, they could make adjustments and still be okay."

6. Make Sure They Have the Proper Training

The number one reason why delegation often fails is the person delegating doesn't have time to train the designee. Make the time to train. If you take the time, you'll only have to train them once and they'll get it right the first time.

I typically like to pick the afternoon to train because it's less hectic. I've finished what I wanted to that day, and it's easier to avoid interruptions.

TIP: If it's a report, show them how to do it (even if you could have done it in the same amount of time yourself) and give them a copy of it.

7. Give the Necessary Authority to the Person You Delegated To

Make sure your designee has the necessary authority to gain access to certain files or to get cooperation from others. Send an e-mail message in advance on behalf of your designee to those whose cooperation will be needed so things will run more smoothly. In your team meeting discuss what tasks or projects you have delegated and to whom, so everyone is on the same page. This will reduce friction and tension as well as improve cooperation among team members.

8. Share the Spotlight and Give Feedback That Encourages

Give them the credit, and let them make the presentation. Getting noticed is a great motivator. This shows that you are proud of them and they're part of the team.

Be sure that if it isn't done the way you asked, you provide constructive criticism and positive motivation, so next time it is done right.

9. Remember—You Are Still Ultimately Responsible

Remember: Even though you delegate the task or project, you must supervise it throughout its completion. You don't want to micromanage, but you do want to follow the progress of the project or task. Even though you've delegated the task or project, you're still the one responsible in the end.

QUICK TIPS

✓ Delegation is one of the highest forms of motivation known.

✓ Your team is only as good as its weakest member.

✓ Focus on the tasks that you're being paid to do as a manager.

✓ The number one skill of great managers is the ability to train others.

✓ Give direct reports the chance to feel part of the team.

✓ Use your calendar or notebook to keep track of the tasks you're delegating.

✓ Tell the person you're delegating to why you've chosen him or her and why the task is so important to you.

✓ Be sensitive to your direct reports' feelings.

✓ Define the task or project as well as you can along with your expectations to eliminate misunderstandings.

✓ Give them an example of the way you've done it in the past.

✓ Give a start date and a deadline, and set up a meeting halfway in between to check their progress.

✓ Accept that others can do it as well as you can, or in some cases better.

✓ Make sure they have the proper training.

✓ Make sure that they don't have any questions and they understand exactly what you want.

✓ Give them the necessary authority to access any information and help that they need.

✓ If possible, delegate the whole task, not just the part you don't want to do.

✓ Share the spotlight, and offer constructive feedback.

✓ Give them sufficient time to complete the task or project.

✓ Try to make sure they are successful so you build up their confidence and your own.

✓ Remember, you are still ultimately responsible.

10

Planning and Executing an Effective Meeting

Conductors of great symphony orchestras do not play every
musical instrument; yet through leadership the ultimate pro-
duction is an expressive and united combination of tones.

—THOMAS D. BAILEY

It seems like everywhere I go today, people have meetings to have meetings, if you know what I mean. Ninety percent of business-people surveyed said that half the time they spend in meetings could have been spent doing more productive tasks, and the average employee loses 31 hours a month in unproductive meetings. Yet why do so few companies (that are supposedly so efficient) spend time and effort improving the quality of their meetings? Let's look at some easy ways to increase the cost-benefit relationship of your next meeting.

This chapter is broken into three parts:

1. How to more effectively plan your meetings so you need fewer meetings to accomplish your desired outcome.

2. How to facilitate and control your meeting so it:
   - Engages your participants
   - Starts on time, sticks to the agenda, and finishes on time
3. How to achieve the objective you established at the beginning of your meeting by the end of your meeting so your meeting actually accomplished something.

CHARACTERISTICS OF UNPRODUCTIVE MEETINGS

- They're longer than necessary.
- More are needed to get the desired results.
- No one received an agenda in time to prepare for the meeting.
- There is a high level of frustration or multiple misunderstandings.
- Information is poorly managed, and there is poor follow-up after the meeting.
- There are more meetings, and therefore less time to work on veggies.
- No one is assigned to take minutes or notes.
- Leader loses control of the meeting.

THERE ARE THREE TYPES OF MEETINGS

1. Informational
2. Decision making or problem solving
3. Brainstorming

PLANNING AN EFFECTIVE MEETING

Do You Really Need to Schedule This Meeting?

Before you schedule your next meeting, ask yourself, "Is this meeting really necessary? Am I just having a meeting because we always have one? Are there enough items or issues to cover to make it worthwhile?" Have you ever considered how much it costs to get everybody together? Maybe you wouldn't have even scheduled the meeting.

I have found that many times, people choose the wrong communication vehicle to achieve their goal. Some examples are:

- They choose Instant Messaging or send e-mails back and forth every few minutes, when they should have called the other person or scheduled a meeting.
- They schedule a meeting or conference call to keep everyone informed (with no discussion when they should have sent an e-mail to the appropriate people.

TIP: If you see e-mails going back and forth, suggest a face-to-face meeting or phone call, which would actually save time and improve communication.

Define Your Desired Outcome

The desired outcome of the meeting determines:

- When to schedule it
- Who to invite
- How long it should take

Seventy-five percent of respondents said they rarely thought about their desired outcome before scheduling a meeting. They schedule a meeting in the morning because that's when it's always been scheduled, invite as many people as they can get to come, and never time the agenda to see how long it will take to cover the items on the agenda. Using clear thought will automatically improve the productivity of your next meeting.

Ask Participants to Submit Ideas or Topics for the Agenda

Get everyone involved. Your participants can often provide ideas you never thought of. This will give them a stake in the meeting and increase the probability they will:

- Show up on time or early
- Be prepared to share pertinent information and ideas

This involvement and preparation should help your meeting achieve the desired outcome and finish on time or early.

Limit the Objectives of Your Meeting and Add Breaks

Short, to-the-point meetings are the most effective. Try to limit your meeting to one hour or less. The average person's attention span is 60 to 90 minutes, yet the clear majority of meetings are longer than 90 minutes. Have you ever looked around the meeting after 60 minutes and noticed participants disengaging or "checking out"? If your meeting goes more than an hour, ask yourself what you could do next time to limit the objectives.

I'm constantly amazed at the length of agendas I see and the amount of time there is to cover the material. The participants would have to speak at 78-rpm speed to cover everything on the agenda. The meeting is guaranteed to finish late. Remember that meeting participants always appreciate meetings that finish early. They'll remember you positively when deciding whether to come the next time you schedule a meeting.

TIP: Next time you make your agenda, eliminate the lowest 20 percent of your agenda, and you might finish on time or early.

Have an Agenda and Distribute It Early

I'm embarrassed to tell you how many meetings I've been to or researched over the last 20 years that had no agenda. A meeting without an agenda is a tip-off that the meeting is going to be a "bull session," run long, and have a limited benefit. I finally learned this lesson and made this rule: if I didn't get an agenda in time to prepare, I didn't come to the meeting unless the leader was the president or CEO of the company. I didn't have the time to waste in unproductive meetings. Remember: If you don't respect your time, who will?

So be sure to give everyone plenty of time to organize their schedules so they can attend your meeting. Chances are that you'll get a much better turnout. Participants can organize and prepare before the meeting, which will keep the meeting short.

TIP: Ask others to give you an agenda so you can be prepared to contribute to their meeting (and see if you really need to be there or can send someone else).

Let Participants Know Why They've Been Invited

Many people say they don't know why they were invited to a particular meeting. In addition, they don't receive an agenda before the meeting; they often don't know who else is invited; and thus they don't prepare properly for the meeting.

Tell each participant why you've invited them and what you expect from each of them at the meeting. This will encourage them to come, show how you value their participation, and increases the chances they will be prepared.

ORGANIZE YOUR AGENDA AND MEETING THIS WAY

- One-sixth of the meeting should cover your introduction and minutes from the last meeting (10 minutes of a 60-minute meeting).
- Four-sixths of the meeting should cover the items on your agenda (40 minutes of a 60-minute meeting).
- One-sixth of the meeting should put closure on the meeting by summing up the meeting, going over action items for the next meeting, and setting up a date and time for the next meeting (10 minutes of a 60-minute meeting).

Cover the Most Important Issues First

Use the veggie principle to prioritize your agenda. People are freshest at the beginning of a meeting. Cover the most important items on your agenda first. That way, if people are called away or you run out of time, it won't matter as much because the important items on the agenda have already been covered. This will really help you finish the meeting on time.

Many agendas do the opposite. They start out with the easy items (so they can get them out of the way), and the meeting is guaranteed to run long because the most important issues are left to discuss when the meeting is supposed to be over.

Have Starting and Ending Times

Just a hint: Don't schedule your meeting to begin on an even hour, like 2 p.m. People may perceive your meeting as starting around 2 p.m. When you say 2:10 p.m., however, people will know that you mean 2:10 p.m. Worst case: if they thought your meeting started at 2 p.m. and they show up at 2:10 p.m., they'll still be on time.

TIP: Close the door and begin at the specified time. Let latecomers know it's not okay to be late. Establish "fines" for latecomers. Respect your time and the time of those who came at the scheduled meeting time.

Have Ground Rules for Your Meetings

Companies should establish ground rules for all their meetings. These ground rules should be published in a visible location in each meeting room. This will create the appropriate standards and structure for each meeting. Many very effective companies already do this, but it's surprising how many don't.

CHAPTER 10

If that isn't the case at your company, publish ground rules before your meeting or write them on the white board in the front of the room. Go over the ground rules first so that everyone's clear. (After doing this a certain number of times, you can stop doing this if it becomes too repetitious.)

Some examples of ground rules:

- Turn off cell phones, BlackBerries, and so on.
- Don't bring other work to the meeting.
- Go for focus, momentum, and achieving your objective.
- Don't cancel at the last minute (you must send someone in your place).
- Everyone should be prepared to share.
- Everyone's opinion matters.
- Everyone is to be treated with respect.
- Get there early so you can talk with other participants, prepare, or get food and/or beverage before the meeting begins.

TIP: Let participants set and agree to the ground rules. This will increase the chances they will observe them. It will also cut down on interruptions and conflicts that cause the meeting to finish late.

Get to the Room Early

There are several excellent reasons why you should get to your meeting room early:

1. You're not stressed out by arriving at the last minute.

2. You can get comfortable with the room by setting up the room the way you like it. Do you want it in U-shape, round tables, classroom, or conference style? In addition, this will give you time to straighten the chairs and clean up any miscellaneous items.

3. You can put name tents where you want your participants to sit.

4. Because participants say they value a meeting leader who gets to a meeting before them. It shows he or she values their time and is a good planner.

LET THE MEETING BEGIN

Greet Participants When They Arrive

By arriving early, you can get everything set up and stand by the door so you can greet each person as they arrive. This way you can get a "read" on each person as they arrive. Are they looking forward to the meeting or complaining that they have to be there? Do they seem relaxed, excited, or blah? Do you get an impression they are prepared for the meeting and looking forward to sharing? You can tell a lot about a person by really paying attention.

Start Your Meeting with a Thank You

Show your participants that you value their time by thanking them for giving up their time to come to the meeting, the time it took to prepare for your meeting, and for coming to your meeting on time.

Acknowledge that you know they already have a lot of other work to accomplish and it means a lot that they came to your meeting.

Acknowledge that because of this you are going to do everything you can to not waste a minute of their time and finish the meeting on time or early. Participants love to be acknowledged and feel respected.

Set the Tone for the Meeting in the First Five Minutes

By setting an ending time, people can better schedule their day and fit your meeting in. Try to finish your meeting early so that you don't have to use all your allotted meeting time.

When people come late to a class that I teach, I make an example of the student and ask him or her to sit in the front of the room. (How could you be late for a time-management class anyway?) I do it in the form of humor, and the person gets the point. Believe me, word gets around.

Get Everyone Involved from the Beginning

One way to get everyone involved is to go around the room and ask everyone to say their name, department, why they are there, and what they want to get out of the meeting. The sooner you get everyone involved the better the sharing will get.

By getting people to share quickly you can get a read on how quiet or how outspoken they are and their level of enthusiasm for being at your meeting.

To get the meeting going, call on those participants you know like to share. They will help get the meeting going and help you build momentum. Once you get the meeting going, shift the dependence to others who haven't had a chance to share.

Even though the outgoing participants got the meeting going and will probably want to keep sharing, make it a point to make sure everyone shares by calling on the other participants. Try to keep everyone engaged.

Bring Up Items from the Last Meeting First

Discuss the action items from the last meeting first. Good minutes will make people accountable, and follow-up will make people pay attention at the meeting. Taking too long to cover the action items from the previous meeting is one of the easiest ways to lose control of a meeting. Unless you keep the meeting moving, you won't be able to cover everything on your agenda in the time allotted.

Cover Only the Topics on the Agenda

The number one reason why meetings don't finish on time is that the leader of the meeting loses control of the meeting. Be the Ringmaster so that the meeting sticks to the agenda. A meeting that sticks to the agenda will finish faster, and the next time you schedule a meeting, people will be far more likely to attend. It also presents an organized and professional image.

I'm constantly amazed at how many respondents say that many of the meetings they go to have no real Ringmaster. They also explain how frustrating this is to them. If you have to, take turns being the Ringmaster.

TIP: If other issues come up, write them down on a flip chart; and if there's time at the end of the meeting, you can discuss them. Otherwise, you can save them for the next meeting or schedule another meeting to discuss them.

Use a Flipchart to Engage and Control Your Group

I recommend multiple flipcharts in every meeting room. I use a flipchart so I can:

- Write down ideas participants share.
- Park ideas that are brought up but not on the agenda so you can keep control of the meeting.
- Have participants break into teams and use a flip chart to write their ideas down.

When you are trying to generate ideas or options, it's easy to get everyone involved by breaking your group into teams and giving each team a flipchart to write their ideas on. This will also generate more ideas (that are often different), in less time.

A CASE STUDY

Frank hated meetings. They never finished on time. They all seemed to start well for the first few topics, then someone would bring up something that wasn't on the agenda that he or she wanted to talk about. Next thing you knew, the meeting left the agenda; and by the time the discussion was done, they were an hour behind schedule. There goes my day again, he thought.

He decided one day to stand up for his feelings of frustration. He asked his boss if he could volunteer to be the meeting "timer" and for the power to keep the meeting on agenda. His boss agreed to try it for one meeting to see if it would work.

They were all amazed at the results. The first meeting they tried it, they actually finished on time and covered all the topics on the agenda.

Give Assignments to Participants

Make it a team event by giving assignments so that everyone is a part of the meeting. That will get everyone involved and keep them alert.

Possible roles for participants:

- Leader (the Ringmaster): This person is a facilitator and makes sure the meeting sticks to the agenda.
- Note taker: This person takes the meeting minutes.
- Timer: This person makes sure the meeting keeps to specific time limits.
- Tone observer: This person looks for anger or frustration.
- Door person: This person shuts the door when the meeting begins, sits near the door during the meeting, and advises latecomers what's already been discussed.
- Meeting survey taker: This person fills out the meeting survey and critiques how well the meeting met its objectives.

Get people involved in your meeting as quickly as you can by asking them to share something like their name, their position, or what they are responsible for talking about at the meeting. This gets the participants engaged and makes the meeting more interesting for everyone.

Keep Minutes

If you don't keep meeting minutes (which many don't), chances of action items being completed by the next meeting are very poor. Minutes are a key ingredient of a productive meeting and accountability.

Often, minutes are used as a reference and are reviewed before the meeting begins and at the beginning of the next meeting. It's important that everyone agrees with what happened at the meeting. If you are taking notes and minutes for a meeting:

1. Make a list of the participants before the meeting (so you can check them off when they arrive at the meeting).
2. Be familiar with the items on the agenda.
3. Follow the agenda.
4. Write down the formal items (such as time, date, leader, and purpose).
5. Don't write down everything, only key points that relate to the agenda.
6. Ask questions if there is something discussed that you don't understand.
7. Write up and distribute the minutes right after the meeting.

Don't Take Sides

Remember, one of the most important jobs a good facilitator has is to not take sides. You must remain impartial and guide participants to share their thoughts, ideas, and opinions. You need to set up a "safe" environment where participants feel comfortable enough to contribute their ideas. If you don't think you can do this, either appoint an impartial facilitator or try to work out a solution.

Generate Ideas and Build Consensus

Consensus is the cooperative development of a decision that is acceptable enough so that all members of the group agree to support the decision. Consensus means that everyone in the group has veto power. Once you assure your group that you won't move forward without their approval, participants tend to relax and focus on the issues and ideas. If a participant objects to a decision, it is important to find out why and work through his objection. To have a consensus you must consider all concerns and find the most agreeable course of action.

AT THE END OF THE MEETING

Ask Each Participant for His or Her Recommendations

Don't just agree to schedule another meeting. Make sure that you have made significant progress towards a solution or meeting the objective of your meeting. Go around the room and ask each person for their final recommendation before the meeting ends. Try to narrow the solution to no more than two.

Be sure you summarize the main points of the meeting, any decisions the group made, action items for the next meeting, and assignments for participants.

Give Participants Assignments for the Next Meeting

Make sure you give out action items before the meeting ends. Make sure each participant understands what is expected of him or her for the next meeting. Write them down. Write a follow-up e-mail so they know what they'll be responsible for preparing for the next meeting.

Action items that aren't written down usually don't get done.

Thank Everyone for Their Time and Valuable Input

Showing verbal appreciation at the end of a meeting shows participants that you value their time and the sacrifice they made to be there. It can go a long way toward getting them to come again.

Make Sure Your Meeting Finishes on Time

If you prioritized your agenda properly (by discussing the most important issue first), you should be down to the lesser items on your agenda by the time your meeting is supposed to end.

People are more likely to accept a meeting invitation from a person that finishes a meeting on time or early than someone who constantly allows their meeting to run past the allotted time.

Distribute the Minutes from the Meeting

The job of the note taker is to get the notes from the meeting finalized and e-mailed to all the participants within a day after the meeting (while it's fresh in the note taker's mind), so participants can confirm them or ask for changes.

This will make sure everyone is on the same page and understands their responsibility for the next meeting.

OTHER MEETING IDEAS AND STRATEGIES

Ask, "Do I Really Have to Be There?"

Many times, we go to meetings and wonder why we were asked to come. In your Timekeeping Journal, look at the meetings you attended and answer these questions:

1. If I didn't share at the meeting, did I really have to go?
2. Could I have sent someone else instead?
3. Could I have e-mailed the information they needed to discuss?
4. Did I have to be there the whole duration of the meeting?

Plan Your Meetings in the Afternoon

Remember: the purpose of the meeting determines when you should schedule it. When possible, plan your meeting in the afternoon unless the meeting could really be considered a veggie. Here are some reasons why meetings are better in the afternoon:

1. People are more prepared in the afternoon. They can use lunchtime to catch up and prepare for an afternoon meeting.

2. When people are in morning meetings, they're thinking about all the tasks that are piling up and they can't concentrate 100 percent, so the meeting takes longer. By putting the meeting in the afternoon, participants can get their veggies out of the way in the morning, so they'll have less on their mind.

3. After a morning meeting, it's very difficult to run back and jump into a veggie. It takes time to get started again. In the afternoon, that veggie is already out of the way so you don't have to run back to work.

A CASE STUDY

The marketing department always had their staff meeting first thing in the morning every Monday. That was the way it had always been. Sometimes there were real issues, and other times there weren't.

The meeting was only supposed to last an hour but always seemed to run long. One day, a member of the group asked if they had to always have the meeting on Monday mornings. She felt it was the best time of the week for her to get other important tasks done. She felt the Monday morning meeting was:

- A "bull" session since they really didn't have an agenda.

- A distraction because while she was in the meeting, she was thinking about all of the work that was piling up on her desk.

- A way to procrastinate because when the meeting ended, she would walk and talk all the way back to her desk and bother coworkers.

She asked if they could agree to meet only when they really had something to talk about and move the meeting to Friday afternoons, when people would be motivated to keep the meeting focused. That way, everyone could get on the same page each Friday and get their "marching orders" for next week, increasing the chances they could all get off to a faster start every Monday.

The group agreed. Next Friday, they all agreed that they were impressed by the results. The meeting took half as long, and they got more accomplished.

Eliminate Same-Day Meetings

The rule should be that no same-day meetings are held unless participants have time to prepare. Same-day meetings usually last longer and accomplish less. Distribute your agenda and then schedule the meeting for the next day.

TIP: In a worst-case scenario, if you have to schedule meetings in the morning, schedule them in the late morning right before lunch. Don't schedule them first thing in the morning and kill everyone's productivity. By planning it late in the morning, people will get hungry, which will increase their sense of urgency and focus, and the meeting will finish on time.

Try Not to Schedule Meetings on Mondays

Remember that the purpose of the meeting determines when you should schedule it. Staff meetings are best on Fridays. You have your meeting on Friday so you can review the progress of the group and get everyone on the same page so they can get off to a fast start on Monday.

I am amazed at how many senior managers and CEOs schedule conference calls on Monday morning, the best day of the week, and kill the productivity of their group or company. By killing the best day of the week, it puts pressure on employees during the remaining four days of the week.

Don't Schedule Meetings Back to Back

Look at each attendee's schedule before you schedule your meeting. If they have a meeting before yours, give them adequate time to get to yours. Remember, back-to-back meetings are real productivity killers!

TIP: Consider this: if yours is the second meeting, how mentally available are they going to be for yours after they've just come from a two-hour meeting?

Additional Meeting Tips

1. Send out a reminder 30 minutes before your meeting is going to begin.

2. Excuse yourself if the meeting is running long so you won't be late for your next commitment.

3. Pad your electronic scheduler with an extra 30 minutes after the meeting is supposed to end so you can get something to eat or drink, go to the bathroom, check in, and/or get to your next meeting on time.

4. Block out time on your computer so people can't invite you to a meeting first thing in the morning or during veggie time.

5. Don't schedule conference calls at the end of the day.

6. Be aware of time-zone differences when you schedule conference calls.

7. Use PowerPoint when possible to generate more interest and retention.

QUICK TIPS

✓ The type of meeting determines when to schedule it.

✓ Identify your purpose before you schedule it and prepare the agenda.

✓ Ask yourself, "Do I really need to schedule this meeting?"

✓ Calculate the cost of the meeting before you schedule it.

✓ Ask if you really need to be there and when (e.g., the whole meeting).

✓ See if you can send someone else.

✓ Would an FYI e-mail be better than a meeting?

✓ Only invite people who need to be there, and tell them why.

✓ Ask participants to submit items for the agenda.

✓ Write the objective of your meeting on a flip chart and put it by the door, so when your participants arrive, it's the first thing they see.

✓ Plan as many of your meetings in the afternoon as you can.

✓ Don't schedule meetings first thing in a day.

✓ Distribute your agenda at least a day early so participants can prepare.

✓ State clear objectives on your agenda and limit them.

✓ Start your meeting 10 minutes after the hour and make it last 50 minutes. That way, late comers will be on time.

✓ Use the veggie principle to prioritize your agenda.

✓ Cover only the topics on the agenda.

✓ Be sure to have a flip chart to park ideas or topics that aren't on the agenda so you don't lose control of the meeting.

✓ Have a start and end time, and stick to it no matter what.

✓ The facilitator is supposed to be neutral or impartial.

✓ Give assignments to participants and rotate them.

✓ Assign someone to take notes, write them up, and distribute them. Distribute them no more than one day after the meeting.

✓ Have ground rules that everyone has to follow.

✓ Eliminate same-day or back-to-back meetings.

✓ No bringing other work to meetings. Check your Blackberry at the door.

11

Managing the Phone and Interruptions

Be sure, when you think you are being extremely tactful, that you are not in reality running away from something you ought to face.

—FRANK MEDLICOTT

The definition of an interruption is an activity that stops or temporarily stops another activity. It doesn't say whether the activity is part of your job or not. In fact, interruptions come in varying degrees, from worthwhile to simple "relationship building." Interruptions are part of our job, but they can really ruin a day.

WHY INTERRUPTIONS CAN BE SO DAMAGING

1. They can slow you down a little or completely derail you.
2. When we have more than one interruption back-to-back, we tend to lose focus.
3. They can make it difficult to stay with one task for an extended period and cause us to naturally hop from task to task.

Let's see what we can do.

When We Are Interrupted...

- We stop what we are doing.
- We respond to the interruption.
- The interruption ends, and we go back to what we were doing. But, more often, we are off on a new mission.

With your Timekeeping Journal, you have already taken the first major step to minimizing interruptions. You have identified what they are and when and how they occur. In short, you have identified a pattern, the big picture. Now it's time to do something about it.

TIP: Always evaluate your interruptions. Ask yourself, "Is this truly something I must handle right away?"

CRITERIA FOR A WORTHWHILE INTERRUPTION

- Does it relate to one of my goals, priorities, or key projects?
- Is the request important to the needs of a customer, peer, or team member?
- Is it a time-sensitive request from my team leader or boss?

As you can see, not all interruptions are bad. They're a necessity. If an interruption meets the criteria listed above, stop what you're doing and be as helpful as possible. If it doesn't meet the criteria, try to defer the interruption to a better time when you can batch it with other similar requests. Did you notice the similarity between these criteria and the criteria for prioritizing?

Let's look at some ways to control interruptions:

1. I set up times daily to fight fires and handle interruptions. That way, each interruption takes me less time because I'm focused only on it.
2. Also, realize that there are certain times in a day when interruptions will take less time, like before lunch and at the end of the day.
3. I used to tell my direct reports that if they wanted uninterrupted one-on-one time with me, if they could see me between 11 a.m. and 1 p.m., I wouldn't answer the phone or e-mail. I would just concentrate on what they had to say. That way, I could give what they had to say the proper attention because it was important to me. They really responded well, and it cut down on the "drive-by" visits.

TRY TO CONTROL THE NOISE AROUND YOU

Noise is a tremendous interruption. It's one of the fastest ways to lose focus, making it very difficult to be productive. Do people like to congregate outside your cubicle? Have a team agreement that it's okay to tell each other (without feeling bad) to please keep it down or to use a conference or break room.

Loud voices, speakerphones, and common area noise can really affect your concentration. Have you spoken to common offenders in a polite but firm manner? Have you tried headphones? Protect your veggie time!

A CASE STUDY

Crystal was a hard worker. She had a problem, though. Her cubicle was located in a high-traffic area. There were always people gathering in the aisle outside her cubicle to talk. In addition, the woman on the other side of her cubicle wall had a naturally loud voice and often talked about personal affairs at work.

What could she do? She didn't want to offend her coworkers, but it was really affecting her work. She confided her situation to a friend. Her friend suggested that maybe these people had no idea how the office noise was affecting her. Her friend said, "Why not go to lunch with each one separately and in a non-threatening way explain your situation?"

She gave it a try, and it worked. Many of them had no idea about the noise. The others, when they heard how it affected her, offered to try harder in the future. They all agreed to do a better job of respecting each other's situation.

TURN YOUR MONITOR OR LAPTOP

You may not be able to move the desk in your cubicle, but you can usually move your monitor. Move it so you aren't looking directly at the opening of your cubicle. This is an easy way to increase your focus. Sometimes if you look up to see who is walking by, they will take it as a cue to stop and talk to you. Don't give them a reason to stop. (Keep your head down, if you know what I mean.)

CHAIRS IN YOUR OFFICE

If you have chairs in your office, they were probably originally put there to use while conducting business. Now they've become a "target" for colleagues who visit your office. Don't give them the impression: "Come on in and make yourself comfortable!" Ask yourself, "How much do I use the chairs for business?"

TIP: Put some files in those chairs (maybe the ones sitting on your desk). Visitors get tired of standing after a short while.

A CASE STUDY

A division of a major defense contractor heard an idea about taking their chairs out of their offices, so they decided to try it. The first week after they took the chairs out of their offices, they saw an immediate drop in interruptions. People would say, "Where did your chairs go?"

They discovered that many interrupters prefer a comfortable environment so that they're more comfortable sharing.

HAVE A SELECTIVE OPEN-DOOR POLICY

If possible, keep your door shut during your veggie times, say from 8 to 9 a.m. and from 10 to 11 a.m. Tell people you will be available from 9 to 10 a.m. and after 11 a.m. If they have to come in, it must be your leader or a worthwhile interruption. You'll be sorry if you make exceptions—no one will honor or respect your verbal request. You can keep your door open all afternoon if you want.

I trained my direct reports that if they had to see me during my veggie time, they needed to write down their questions before they got up out of their chair and to be prepared to tell me what they thought the answer was. This was a great way to keep the interruption short and focused. (Most times, my direct reports were actually right, and this strategy built up their confidence.)

TIP: Be sure you discuss this arrangement with your leader and gain his or her approval before you institute your new policy.

REDUCE "DRIVE-BY SHOOTINGS"

If you are a manager try to get out of your office at least three times each morning and go to where your team works before they come to you. See if they have any questions or need anything. That way, you'll be more visible, and you will cut down on the number of "drive-by shootings." You will be the Ringmaster and have more control over the questions and interruptions that come from direct reports.

PUT A SIGN OUTSIDE YOUR CUBICLE

Put a sign on your door that says:

- Do Not Disturb
- Working on a "veggie" (pin up a picture of broccoli outside your cubicle)

- Today's schedule (so they know where you will be and when your veggie times will be)
- Working on a project (please leave your request on this pad)

WORK SOMEWHERE ELSE

If you can't close your door, try to find a vacant office or meeting room. (Be sure to tell as few people as possible where you are.)

TELL PEOPLE

Often, people don't know how busy you are. Start out first thing in the morning and tell your peers what a tough day you have ahead and that you won't be able to get together with them until after 11:30 a.m. Get to them before they get to you.

Also, spend some time educating the biggest time wasters in your office. Explain your new limited open-door policy. Set times when you'll be free, and get them to agree not to interrupt you until then. You must be firm.

Remember that you must use a friendly, tactful approach so people don't become defensive. Also, don't always give people free access to your time. Try suggesting a later time when you can block out the interruptions and give them quality time. Remember, it's all about quality time, not the quantity of time you give others.

TIP: Ask your interrupter, "Will this take more than two minutes, because I'm right in the middle of a high priority project?" If it's going to be longer than that, arrange a more convenient time and try to meet at his or her office.

A CASE STUDY

Stan never used to use the computer to schedule his day. Thus, when people looked at his schedule, it seemed as though he was available, so they scheduled a meeting he needed to attend.

Either he went and the meeting really broke up his day, or he had to tell them he couldn't attend because he had an important deadline. He began to realize that if he didn't value his time, who would? He found out when he blocked off time to finish his important tasks that if his attendance at the meeting was important, they would schedule the meeting at a time that was more to Stan's advantage.

IF YOUR COMPUTER SCHEDULES YOUR TIME...

At the end of each day, block out valuable time to get your veggies done tomorrow before someone else schedules a meeting in your veggie time. Schedule a meeting in your computer, so you can get your important tasks done.

LEARN HOW TO TACTFULLY INTERRUPT

Successful people know when to interrupt so that the other person doesn't even know what happened. The best way to do this is to wait until they take a breath and try jumping in as tactfully as possible. Practice this first before you try it.

STAND UP

The number one nonverbal way to tell someone that it isn't going to be a long conversation is to stand up when they come into your office or cubicle. Try not to lean against the corner of your desk, since it will make it seem like you have more time. You may have to walk out of your cubicle or office if they don't get the message.

ARRANGE A LATER TIME

Explain to interrupters that you'd really like to talk with them, but you're under a tough deadline. Suggest a better time, like after 11:30 a.m. or during a break or lunchtime. Offer to go to their office or their choice of location. Be careful to make sure they don't think you're too good for them, and don't hurt their feelings. This will increase people's perception that you're all about business and very professional, but still respectful of their feelings.

DON'T PROLONG THE INTERRUPTION

Resist the temptation to add your two cents or a similar story to the interruption. You're only going to make it more difficult to end the interruption swiftly. Carefully pick the interruptions you want to prolong.

AGREE TO A GROUP POWER HOUR

Many groups find after looking at their Timekeeping Journals that they're their own biggest interrupters. Groups are now looking at ways to get more productive together.

They pick two times in the morning when they agree to keep the noise and interruptions down to a minimum. They call it a "power hour."

They put up signs saying, "Quiet—you're entering the veggie zone!" People may laugh, but it really works!

TIP: Handle interruptions in teams. This way, you may be able to shelter others in your group so they can get more work done, and then switch off so you can get some work done.

A CASE STUDY

Mary worked in a cubicle environment. She and her teammates sat very close to each other. You could hear everything each one of them said. Mary was very frustrated. She always tried to work hard and stay focused, but the people around her used their speaker phone or talked loudly, gathered outside her cubicle and talked, or popped up every few minutes to tell a story or ask a question. Mary couldn't seem to get anything done without being interrupted.

She didn't want to say anything because she felt people wouldn't like her and she wouldn't be seen as a team player. Finally, though, she brought up the issue to her boss and suggested two group power hours each morning, where everyone would agree to keep it down and cut down on the interruptions.

Her boss brought up the idea at the next staff meeting and backed the idea. Once it was adopted, everyone was amazed at how much more they got done.

DELEGATE THE INTERRUPTION

Often, you're not the appropriate person to answer a question or solve a problem. Resist the temptation to be a "people pleaser," and don't try to solve their problem. Take a quick minute to direct them to the appropriate person. It's faster for the appropriate person to answer their question or solve their problem than it is for you. Be sure you tactfully explain that to them.

MANAGING THE PHONE AND VOICE MAIL

Keep a Phone Log

The first step in getting control of the phone is to keep a running phone log for a week. Write down the time, the person's name, the nature of the call, and the actual time the call took. Look for patterns in the calls you receive. The best time to set aside to work on a veggie is when the number of incoming calls seems lowest. If you could cut two to five minutes off every call you made or received, can you imagine how much time you'd save each day? For many, it could be as much as an hour or more. In evaluating your log, ask yourself these four questions:

1. Which calls were absolutely necessary?
2. Could you delegate any of them in the future?
3. Were any of your calls just wasted time, or were you procrastinating?
4. What could you do in the future to reduce your time on each call?

Outgoing Calls

Before You Pick Up the Phone, Plan Your Call

The number one way to save time on the outbound calls you make is to plan your call before you pick up the phone.

TIP: Ask, "Why am I making this call?" before you pick up the phone. Also ask, "What is my objective or objectives?"

Have a bulleted outline or agenda regarding what you want to accomplish and what you want to talk about in a prioritized order (using the veggie principle) before you pick up the phone. Keep any necessary information at your fingertips. People will get the impression that you're well organized and don't want to waste your time or theirs. If they have caller ID and see your number, they may be more willing to take your call.

Picking up the phone to make a call without a plan is like going to the grocery store without a list of what you need to purchase. (You go up and down every aisle, eating along the way because you're hungry, so it takes longer. You spend more than you intended. When you get home, you realize that you forgot the one item you originally went to the store to get, so you have to go back.) I've had phone calls like that, have you?

A CASE STUDY

Whenever Greg had a thought or idea, needed something, or was simply returning a call, he picked up the phone without much thought.

Sometimes he called people back so quickly that he realized he hadn't even listened to their whole voice mail message. As a result, he didn't answer all their questions. Thus, they would call back again and ask for more information or have more questions.

He also found that when he called people, he seemed to only get their voice mail. Finally, a friend told him the reason. He told Greg he had caller ID, and when he saw Greg's number, normally he would let it go to voice mail. Greg asked him why. His friend said, "When you call me, you're not very focused, and the call seems to go on forever. I don't have the time. I hope I didn't hurt your feelings, but you asked."

He started to keep a log of his incoming and outgoing calls for a week. Greg was stunned: when he looked at his log, he found he was wasting a lot of his own time as well as others'. He was amazed at how much time he could save with a little planning.

Batch Your Calls

Set aside time each day to return calls, especially medium and low-priority calls. Typically, use from 11:30 a.m. to noon and at the end of the day, to return calls. This is part of the Ringmaster principle — focus on one thing at a time and you'll be more effective. Your calls will take less time because you're only making phone calls.

TIP: It's easier to keep the call short and focused before lunch and at the end of the day because people are in a rush to eat or go home.

Prioritize Your Calls

Call back people according to how the call relates to your priorities. Use the veggie principle to determine who to call back first. That way, if you run out of time you will have returned all of the most important calls. The others can wait until your next phone time.

Keep the Call Focused

Lack of focus is the number two reason why phone calls go on forever. State the reason you're calling them first. Have an idea in your mind before you make the call as to how long it should take to cover your main points. Stay on the topic you need to discuss. If the call starts to wander, be the Ringmaster and get it back on track. Here are some effective ways to end your call without offending the other person:

- Tell them someone just walked into your office (like your boss, for example).
- Tell them you have to go to a meeting.
- Tell them there's someone on the other line or you have another call.
- Summarize the call and say, "Does that cover everything?"
- Tell them, "I know you're really busy, so I'm going to let you go." (A personal favorite.)

Check the Clock Before You Pick Up the Phone

Find a clock and check the time before you pick up the phone. Set a goal of how much time you have to complete the call. Keep an eye on the clock so the call and time don't get away from you. Create a sense of urgency for yourself to achieve the goal of your call in your allotted time.

Make Telephone Appointments

Telephone appointments are also good when you reach the right person but he or she is too busy to talk right at that minute, or when a person is hard to reach but you really need to talk to that person. Immediately ask when would be a better time to talk and *write it down.*

Make sure the person also writes down the appointment. This will allow the other person to hopefully prepare for your future call, which will keep the call focused and structured and will reduce the length of time the call takes.

Other Suggestions

- Anticipate possible questions the person you're calling will ask.
- Try to figure out the best time to reach your contact.
- If you can't reach them by phone, don't be afraid to fax or e-mail them a message. If it's really important and you're stuck, go to their office.
- If someone offers to take a message, ask for voice mail. Your message will be more accurate and detailed.
- If you're calling back with or requesting information and don't need to speak with the other person, try to pick a time when he isn't there.

- Make notes on your Master List of what you talk about during the phone call. It might come in handy in the future.

INCOMING CALLS

Find a Way to Screen Your Calls

Successful people use their voice mail or their assistant during veggie time to protect themselves so they can get their veggies accomplished. If you have an assistant, meet first thing in the morning, explain that day's schedule to him or her, and have him or her screen your calls. Your assistant can tell lower priority callers that you're in a meeting or your door is closed, and find out when the best time would be for you to return the call.

If you don't have an assistant, use your voice mail more effectively. Let the call go to voice mail during your veggie time, then check it when you finish your thought or task. That way, you will be the Ringmaster because you'll be deciding the priority of the call.

You can research the answer or information the caller needs, call him or her back, and leave the answer on the person's voice mail without even having to speak to him or her.

If you answer the phone, the call will become the Ringmaster because you'll drop what you're currently doing and try to handle it right away. If it's more important than what you're currently working on, you will need to stop what you're doing, make a note where you are, and take the call.

Otherwise, you can put the message on your Master List and return the call when you finish your veggie. The use of voice mail is discussed more thoroughly later in this book. Of course, if you're in customer service or must answer every call, be sure that you keep the call focused and as short as possible.

Let People Know the Best Time to Reach You

Everyone has to be available to receive calls sometime. Let the people you talk to the most know when the best time is to reach you (and the worst). Give those callers the names of others in your department who can also help them.

Delegate the Call to the Appropriate Person

Often, there may be someone else who could better handle the call because either it's a higher priority for them than it is for you or they have the needed information. Resist the temptation to be a people pleaser. Give the caller the name and number of the correct person, or offer to forward their call to the right person. Explain that it will take less time if the appropriate person handles their call or request.

Quickly Assess the Nature of the Call

Decide how the call relates to your priorities. Is it worth dropping what you're currently working on, or can you call the person back at a time that better fits your schedule and the priority of the call?

Ask the caller, "What can I do for you?" Encourage the caller to get to the point quickly; don't let the caller start talking about the weather. Keep asking questions until you determine the nature of the call.

TIP: Encourage others to plan their calls before they pick up the phone to call you (another Ringmaster strategy). This will help keep the call focused and reduce the chances that they will ramble.

A CASE STUDY

Jackie answered the phone every time it rang. Sometimes the call was very worthwhile, and other times it wasn't. Oftentimes, even when the call was worthwhile, the person calling wasn't prepared so the call seemed to take forever. Jackie didn't want to be impolite, but she had a lot of work to do.

Jackie started thinking. If she really valued her time and wanted to leave work on time, she realized she was going to have to take control of the call much sooner. She realized that the phone was her biggest interrupter. When she started to keep the calls focused, she realized that she could save 30 to 60 minutes a day.

HOW TO USE VOICE MAIL EFFECTIVELY

Many people never change their own voice mail, even if they aren't in the office that day or week. Here are two options that will increase your professionalism:

1. Leave a voice mail message once a week that tells your caller the date of that specific week and your schedule.
2. Leave a new voice mail daily that announces the date and tells the caller your schedule that day.

The Benefits of Changing Your Voice Mail Message

- It will make you sound more professional.
- It will prompt your caller to leave the information you really need to help him or her.
- It gives the caller the impression that voice mail is important to you and that you check it. (It will reduce the chances they'll hit zero and ask the operator to page you or transfer them to another member of your team.)

You can also give the caller some options listed below:

- The name of someone else who they can contact if it's important that they speak to someone immediately.
- Another phone or pager number they can use to reach you immediately.
- They can hit zero and speak to the operator (to be redirected).
- They can still leave a voice mail message.

TIP: By changing your voice mail message, you can respect the caller's time so he or she doesn't wait around for a return call if he or she needs an immediate response.

A CASE STUDY

Gloria hated the phone. She would check voice mail messages and call them back quickly, only to get their voice mail. She realized that she hated phone tag the most. Her favorite message was, "Guess who is calling, guess my phone number, and guess what I want." She wanted to send them a "special" message.

She started to realize, "Maybe I'm part of the problem. If I had a voice mail greeting that told callers what I really needed to help them, maybe I could leave the answer to their question on their voice mail without even talking to them." Since the phone was her biggest time waster, this could really save her some time. Once she started changing her voice mail daily and callers started leaving specific voice mails, she was amazed: she really saved a lot of time every day.

What to Ask for from Your Caller on Your Voice Mail Greeting

- His or her name
- His or her phone number
- The nature or reason for the phone call
- The best time for you to call him or her back if he or she needs to talk. (This will increase the chances that the person will be there when you call so you don't play phone tag.)

How this saves you time:

1. You know the caller's name, so you don't have to guess.
2. You don't have to look up the caller's phone number.
3. You can leave the answer on his or her voice mail without actually talking.

4. You can avoid playing phone tag by getting him or her to tell you when to call back.

When You Leave Voice Mail

Try to leave a detailed voice mail in the same way you're asking them to do for you. This is why I plan my call before I pick up the phone. In today's hectic environment, you should assume that when you call someone, you're going to get his or her voice mail. By having a plan before you call, if you get their voice mail, your message will be shorter and to the point. Leave them all the details discussed above, plus set a deadline for them to respond. Be sure to speak slowly, especially when leaving your phone number, so they can write it down.

TIP: Leave your phone number twice in the message, once at the beginning and once at the end of the message. That way, they won't have to replay your whole message if they missed your phone number the first time they listened to it.

TIP: Don't leave messages longer than 30 seconds, if possible. Otherwise, they may only respond to part of your message or none at all.

Other Voice Mail Tips

1. If you're calling them back with information they requested and don't need to talk, pick a time when they won't be there. (It'll cut down on the conversation time.)

2. If you're requesting information and don't need to talk, suggest they e-mail you with the information you need.

3. Return all voice mail within 24 hours, if possible, even if it's after hours and you know they're not there. (Perhaps explain the circumstances as to why you couldn't call sooner.)

4. If you get a voice mail from a salesperson and you're not interested, call back and leave a voice mail that politely says that you're not interested or you'll call when you are. (This will reduce your voice mail in the future and make you seem more professional.)

QUICK TIPS

✓ Ask yourself, "Is this truly something I must handle right away?"

✓ Put a picture of a veggie outside your cubicle or office if you're working on an important task or project.

✓ Close your door when you are working on a veggie or need to really concentrate. Try not to keep it closed for more than an hour.

✓ If you are a manager or leader try to get out of your office at least three times a day and visit your direct reports in their environment.

✓ Tell your biggest interrupters first thing in the morning that you have a difficult day ahead and that you may not be able to get with them until lunch time.

✓ Work in a conference room and shut the door to avoid interruptions.

✓ Ask others before interrupting them, "Do you have a minute?" Ask others to do the same for you.

✓ Block out time on your computer to get important tasks done.

✓ If you can't handle a question or request right away, offer to go see them when you finish what you're working on so you control the interruption.

✓ Don't prolong the interruption.

✓ Suggest setting up a group power hour at your next team meeting.

✓ If you're not the right person, delegate the interruption to the right person.

✓ Set up times to make outbound calls (batching).

✓ Use the veggie principle when making calls.

✓ Plan your call before you pick up the phone.

✓ Keep your call focused so it stays on track. Keep an eye on the clock when talking.

✓ Make telephone appointments when necessary.

✓ Screen your calls during veggie time.

✓ Let others know the best time to reach you and how.

✓ Get your caller to get to the point as quickly as possible.

✓ Change your voice mail greeting daily or weekly so it tells the caller your schedule.

✓ Leave short 15- to 30-second messages for others.

✓ Speak slowly when leaving messages. Leave your phone number twice.

12

Developing a Simple, Effective Filing System

A place for everything, and everything in its place.

—proverb

A clear desktop reduces the likelihood of self-interruptions; but when our desks are cluttered, we lose focus. On the average, 45 minutes are lost every day hunting for information (paper) on and in our desks. And more and more often, employees are being evaluated on how their workspace looks. If your piles have names, you might have a problem.

TIP: Think of yourself as a jukebox. A jukebox takes out a CD, plays the selected song or songs, and then puts it back. Then it gets another.

Many people are afraid that a file out of sight is a file out of mind. But if you want to add focus and concentration to your work habits, try to only have one file open on your desk at a time. This way, there aren't any other files on your desk to distract you. The point is, by having one file on your desk at a time, you increase your ability to focus, and your task or project will take less time to complete with fewer mistakes.

Many people use the top of their desk as their to-do list. In fact, many times their piles actually have names. Remember, though, that you won't take those piles off your desk until two things happen:

1. You can keep the task or tasks you need to complete in each file in front of your eyes by using a Master List or calendar.
2. You can find your files quickly in your file drawer.

AN EXAMPLE

At my son's Montessori school, if you want to play with a different toy, you have to put away the toy you currently have before you can get another one. I bet that's a tough sell!

The key to gaining focus and concentration is to only have one thing on your desk at a time. By bringing 100 percent of your focus and concentration to bear on one task or project that task or project will take less time and you'll make fewer mistakes.

Below are some easy steps to gain control of your desk. They are to be done in this order.

TAKE EVERYTHING OFF YOUR DESK

Pretend you just moved into your office or cubicle. Take everything off your desk and put it on the floor next to everything else that's already there. Get out the spray cleaner and thoroughly wipe off your desk. Now, put things back on top of your desk in order of what you use most. To improve my focus and concentration, the following is what I did, and didn't, put back on the top of my desk.

Items I Put Back on My Desk

- The monitor, keyboard, and mouse for my computer
- My phone (If you're right handed, it should go on the left side of your desk. If you're left handed, place it on the right side of your desk.)
- My lamp
- My pen and pencil holder
- My calculator
- A clock
- A plant (dead does not qualify)
- An in-basket
- Blotter

Things I Didn't Put Back on My Desk

- Personal pictures (they distract you)
- Additional stacking in-baskets
- Candy
- Pen and pencil cup
- Piles of paper and files

In order to gain focus and concentration, you must ask yourself, "Is there anything I could do without?" Get rid of all the clutter. Remove old outdated items. Put your pictures out of your immediate sight. You can either put your pictures behind you if you have a credenza, to the side of your immediate vision, or above you if you are in a cubicle.

People ask me all the time, "Why do I have to move my pictures out of my direct line of vision?" The answer is, when I had pictures on my desk, it was one of the easiest ways to procrastinate. I would look at my pictures and daydream. I would imagine myself in the picture, on the beach, at that wonderful resort. Do you get the picture? You want to eliminate anything distracting, so it's just you and your veggie task or project. That way, it will take less time to complete it.

HAVE A CLOCK VISIBLE

Keep the clock in front of you to make you aware of time. It should be a clock that gets your attention. Your perception of how long tasks/activities take and the actual time they took to complete are often two different things. I put my clock between my two biggest interrupters, my phone and my laptop or monitor, so I can keep track of the amount of time I spend on each. This is how I use my clock to keep my day moving:

1. When the phone rings, I look at the clock, answer the phone, begin talking, and keep my eye on the clock. It helps me keep the call short and focused.

2. When I check and respond to e-mail, I only do it for a set period of time, then I close my e-mail again and get back to my other work.

3. When people walk into my office, I look at the clock. After a reasonable period of time, I try to sum up things so I can get back to work.

4. I set up specific times to work on my veggies and fires.

5. I use the clock to get the majority of my work done before noon.

6. I use the clock to try to leave work on time.

A CASE STUDY

Everyday seemed the same to Joan. She would get to work, start working, and the next thing she knew it was time to go home. She used to say, "Where did the day go?"

She then realized that the clock on her wrist and the one on her computer really didn't help her have the discipline she needed to stay on track all day long. She needed a clock that was big enough to get her attention so she could see where her time was going.

Now, when interruptions start she looks at the clock and gets a point of reference. After what seems to be about five minutes, she looks over at the clock and excuses herself. She realized that she had to keep moving or she would lose any hope of leaving on time. Now Joan is much more focused and in control and gets more accomplished.

ORGANIZE YOUR TOOLS

- Empty your desk.
- Go through and cut down on pens, pencils, paper clips, and so on. Do you have enough supplies to open your own Office Depot? Only keep a 30-day supply.
- Divide your drawers into different areas, e.g., stationery, files, and personal.
- Throw away the stuff that mysteriously appeared in your desk.

REMOVE THE FUTURE AND PAST FROM YOUR DESK FILE

The first step is to organize the files that are in the file drawers in your desk. If you want to overcome paper overload, only manage the "present" (what you're currently working on over the next 30 days).

TIP: The "present" is the most important. Treat your desk and desk-top like valuable real estate. Only keep what you're currently working on close by. In the file drawers located in your desk, remove the two following types of files and put them on the floor for the time being.

The Past

These are files that have been completed or closed out. The only reason you're going to use them in the future is for reference.

The Future

If you find a file and say to yourself, "Someday I just might need this," or "Someday I'd like to read this," remove it and put it on the floor. At the end, you will put it in your reference file.

A CASE STUDY

Brad was getting very frustrated. He needed a shoehorn to get another file into the file drawers in his desk. He sent his boss an e-mail. He asked, "Would it be all right to order another file cabinet? I don't have any more room in my file drawers."

His boss asked him to go through the file drawers in his desk and make sure everything was absolutely necessary. If it wasn't necessary, Brad was to either put it in reference or throw it way.

He grudgingly did what his boss asked. "What a waste of time," he thought. He started looking at one file at a time. If the file was something he had already finished or something he didn't think he would get to for a while, he put it on the floor (next to the files that were already there).

When he got done, he looked at his two file drawers. He realized he had 50 percent more room now. He discovered that he had solved his paper overload problem. He may not be able to manage the past, present, and future, but he could manage the present by itself.

HOW TO SET UP YOUR WORKING FILES

Set up your working files in the drawer(s) located in your desk. Organize your files alphabetically or chronologically. These files should typically be at arm's length, either in your desk or very close by. Remember, keep your system simple. Here are some suggestions for setting up a successful working file system.

Suggestions for Setting Up Working Files

- Fingertip info: Phone lists, addresses, and frequently used information
- Current projects: Set up files for each separate project
- Routine tasks: Performed daily, weekly, or monthly
- Clients or prospects
- Problems or issues to be researched

Limit the Number of Categories by Keeping Them Broad

If you have too many categories, you won't be able to quickly find a file anyway. Try to have no more than 7 to 10 categories.

A CASE STUDY

Karen was the assistant to the CEO of a large corporation. Everyone admired her organizational skills. She never had anything on her desk. She seemed so organized.

Karen had a secret, though. She had over 30 categories, and it was very difficult to find things quickly. She was constantly making duplicate copies and putting them in different categories. She then realized she needed a simpler system.

She wrote down the name of each category. Then she looked for common factors between her categories. After her first pass, she cut down to 15 categories, then 10. She felt much more comfortable with a simple file system that made it faster to find files in the heat of the moment.

Create File Names That Make It Easy to Find Your Files

Before you pick a name for a file, think of where you would look for it again in the future if you had to find it quickly. Make your file names interesting.

Don't Put Too Many Papers in Each Folder

Too many papers in a folder will slow you down because you might not find what you're looking for on the first pass. Weed your folders out weekly, and start a new folder if you have to.

Get Honest About What You Really Need

When was the last time you looked at the information you're keeping? Is it outdated? You can only realistically manage so much. If you didn't look at it this week, what are the chances you'll look at it next week? Too much will only slow you down.

TIP: Every Friday, go through your files and see if you have any duplicates or ones you have finished. Throw away extra paper and put files in the reference file located across the room so you're ready for next week.

How to Determine Your File Categories

Take out a piece of paper. Look at each of the files on your desk and the ones left in your drawer. Make a note about the topic of each. When you're done, see if there is a way to break them down into 7 to 10 categories.

A CASE STUDY

Ralph was really behind on his filing. He kept saying, "Some Saturday I'm going to come in to work and file all of this." Every Saturday, though, something seemed to come up. One day he realized, "Maybe if I just work on this a little each day, I could get caught up." He realized he hated filing as much as going to the dentist.

So, the next day, he broke his piles into smaller stacks that didn't seem as difficult. He scheduled 30 minutes at the end of each day to work on filing just one pile a day. He realized, after he finished a pile each day that he felt a little more in control and actually began to look forward to coming to work more the next day. Once he got the present filed, he worked on the past and then the future. He still has never gone back to leaving piles on his desk. He wondered why he hadn't thought of it sooner!

Separate the Papers and Folders into 5 to 10 Piles

One reason why we put off filing is that our piles are usually large and overwhelming. Make your piles smaller so that you can talk yourself into filing a little each day at the end of the day. If you have a lot of files, you may want to make more than 10 piles. What's an extra week if you've already put off filing for this long?

At one point in my career, it seemed like I was a year or more behind in my filing. It felt hopeless. Then I broke my piles of paper and files into 30 smaller piles. Every day I worked on just filing a little, at the end of each day. I had everything filed in a month. Since that day when I finished that last pile, I've never gone back to having piles on my desk.

Bring Out the Garbage Can and Make It Your Friend

Place the garbage can next to you and be prepared to fill it.

Purchase Colored File Folders

Each category in your working files will have a different color. By using different colors, you'll be able to go to the category you want more quickly. The fastest way to file is to use visual aids like colored file folders. The eye can pick up the colors much faster.

Get a Box of Manila Folders and a Bold Pen

You're going to create a little assembly line. Each time you pick up a piece of paper that needs a new manila folder, reach in the box and grab one. Then take your Sharpie bold marker, write your file name on it, and put the file into the file drawer in your desk.

Handle Paper Only Once

Once you touch a file or piece of paper in one of your stacks, it can't go back to where it came from. It must go in one of the five following places:

- The garbage
- The future
- The past
- The present
- Outbound (sign off on it, or delegate it to someone else)

That file or piece of paper can't be placed back on your desk. (Many times, that's why our piles don't get smaller. The paper just goes back into a new pile on our desk.) These five options eliminate questions and the need for new piles.

TIP: When you first look at a piece of paper, make a note on the top what file it should go in. This will save you time reevaluating it again later. Next time you pick it up, you'll already know where it goes.

A CASE STUDY

Maria always had the best intentions. It seemed like she filed on a regular basis, but one day she realized she still had quite a few piles on her desk. She thought to herself, "I have to get this under control!"

One day, she picked up a pile and began separating it. She picked up the first piece of paper and thought, "Where does this go?" She laid it back down and declared, "New file category." The same thing happened with the next piece of paper. Then she looked at the third piece of paper and thought, "I don't know where you go," and laid it down. The fourth piece of paper didn't even belong to her. This went on for some time until she realized she now had many separate piles.

She then gathered them all together again and moved them to another part of her desk. She then realized the problem. The piles were simply moving in a circular fashion on her desk but never really going away. She made herself a deal. From now on, if she picked up a piece of paper or a file, it couldn't go back to where it had come from. It had to go in one of the five choices listed previously. She never had this problem again.

STOP USING POST-ITS

If you stop for a second, you'll realize these only add to clutter. It often takes as long to find information written on a Post-it as it would have if we hadn't written it down at all. Use your Master List as one central location for all your notes. *Note:* You may have to slowly wean yourself off the Post-its, so be gentle.

Put the Future and the Past in the Reference File

This is the last step because it's the lowest priority. Take the future and the past files and put them in your reference files. This is the tall, four-drawer file located in the corner of your office or cubicle. These files contain research for future projects and past projects you have completed. They will typically require three drawers for the past and one for the future.

File a Little Every Day So It Won't Get Out of Hand

Every time you start a new project, create a file right then. Don't let filing build up.

TIP: Make it a regular habit to file as you go or at the end of each day, and use Friday afternoon to finish for the week.

Leave Work Every Day with a Clean Desktop

Put those files away! Tomorrow is another day. Your Master and Daily Lists should be about the only things left on your desk. Here are the benefits:

- You'll be ready to do battle and get off to a fast start when you come in tomorrow. (It's very difficult to get off to a fast start first thing in the morning when you come into work and your desk looks like a tornado hit it.)
- You'll feel more in control.
- You'll have more focus.

- Your confidential or sensitive files will be kept private.
- If there was a fire and the sprinklers went off, your files would be safe from water damage.

QUICK TIPS

✓ Keep a clear desktop. The average person loses 45 minutes a day looking through papers and Post-its.

✓ Only have one thing on your desk at a time. Only take out something new after you've put the other file away.

✓ Don't use the top of your desk as your to-do list.

✓ Take everything off your desk, pretend you just moved in and this is your first day, and put only the things you use the most on your desktop.

✓ Have a very visible clock on your desk so you can see where your time is going.

✓ Focus on organizing the present first. Don't worry about the future or the past until everything else is organized.

✓ Limit the number of categories you have to 10, or you won't be able to find a file anyway.

✓ Create file names that are no more than three words long and that are written in large letters so the file is easy to find. Don't put too many papers in each manila file folder.

✓ Purchase colored file folders to make your categories stand out.

✓ Use a bold Sharpie marker to write your file names.

✓ When you first handle a piece of paper, make a note on it stating which category it belongs in. Stop using Post-its as to-dos. Use your Master List instead.

✓ Put the future and the past in the tall four-drawer reference file located in the corner of or outside your office. File a little at the end of each day so it doesn't get out of hand.

✓ Make sure you put everything away before you leave work so you can get off to a fast start tomorrow.

13

Finding Two More Hours a Day

*We shall never have more time. We have, and have always had,
all the time there is. No object is served in waiting until next
week or even until tomorrow. Keep going day in and out.
Concentrate on something useful. Having decided to achieve a
task, achieve it at all costs.*

—ARNOLD BENNETT

Would you like to find two more hours a day? Did I get your attention? Two hours equals 120 minutes. When you are trying to find 120 more minutes a day you need to realize they aren't all in one place. You lose 15 minutes here (trying to find something), 30 minutes there (handling an interruption you lost control of). You get the idea. I put this chapter at the back of the book because after reading the previous chapters you will have a better, more accurate idea where you are losing time throughout your day. The purpose of this chapter is to look through that Timekeeping Journal and using the strategies discussed in the previous chapters, discover ways you can improve what you accomplishing each day.

CHAPTER 13

THE LAW OF SUBTRACTION

If you're currently leaving work each night at 7 p.m. and you want to be able to leave on time, say 5 p.m., you have to figure out a way to eliminate two hours' worth of activities. You won't find all two hours in one place. It will be more like 5 minutes here and 10 minutes there. When you add it all up, it can be two hours or more. A great place to start is in the morning. You have to examine how you're spending your time each day to find ways to subtract minutes.

The key I've found is to be brutally honest. This was difficult for me to do at first because I was already successful. But the real question should be, "Do you want to stay until 7 p.m. every night or do you want to go home and have a personal life?"

My mission statement was that I wanted to watch my two small children grow up. That caused me to have to make some difficult choices. I had to value my time at work more. I had to look for ways to organize and control myself and my day more effectively; otherwise, I'd never get out of work on time. This made it easier for me to create a sense of urgency every day.

If, in the back of your mind, you tell yourself you can always fall back on 5 to 7 p.m., how can you create a sense of urgency? The answer is, you can't. Every Friday, when I reviewed what I had done that week, I looked for ways I could improve the following week. Each week, I accomplished a little more in less time. After a year, my life was much different. The key is that you must be willing to embrace change and look for opportunities to save time.

Here are some tools you can use:

• Your Timekeeping Journal

- Your Master List and Daily List
- Typical fires (interruptions and unplanned events/tasks)

As you look at each activity that shows up in your journal or on your list, ask these two questions:

1. Was working on that task or activity the best use of my time?
2. Was I doing the right task at the right time?

WHEN YOU REVIEW YOUR JOURNAL

By now, I hope you have completed the Timekeeping Journal exercise downloadable from the Website http://www.kztraining.com/timekeepingjournal/. If so, you will find a wealth of insights by reviewing what you recorded. Ask yourself:

- Which activities could be eliminated? (Did they just waste your time?)
- Which activities could I reduce the length of time spent on?
- Which activities could I have delegated?
- Which activities could I have batched with other similar ones?

Take an honest look at each activity you've recorded and identify how you could reduce the amount of time you spend on that type of activity in the future.

How can you use the organizational skills you learned in the previous two chapters to save time by organizing your tasks and projects more effectively? Remember: the morning is usually the time when the fastest improvement can be made.

TIP: The key for most people is to examine the morning. If you're a morning person, that's when you will find the biggest productivity gains. If you aren't a morning person, look at the afternoon.

How could you set up each day more effectively so you could get off to a faster start, have more discipline, and get more done in the morning? Could you move any activities to the afternoon of the previous day?

A CASE STUDY

Tim always thought he was great at managing his time. He always seemed busy. He thought, "There's no way I could save two hours or more per day."

After he kept track of his time for a week, he was amazed at how many interruptions he had every day. At the end of each day, he added up how many tasks he started and how many he completed. No wonder he felt like a great starter but a poor finisher. He realized that was why he was falling further and further behind.

He realized when he looked at each activity or event on his sheet that he could probably save 5 minutes here, 10 minutes there. He found he could actually save more than two hours per day, but that it wasn't in one place in his day.

ACTIVITY

Look through the Time Journal you filled out at the beginning of this book and answer these questions:

1. Which activities could be eliminated?
2. Which activities could I reduce the amount of time I spent on?
3. Which activities could be delegated?
4. Which activities could be batched more effectively?
5. How could you get more accomplished in the morning?

Be prepared to share your answers with your team and/or the rest of the class.

QUICK TIPS

✓ You will never have more time, so make the most of what you currently have. If you want to go home on time daily, look for activities you can eliminate.

✓ As you look at each task you work on, look for ways to save time.

✓ Are there any tasks you're doing yourself that could be delegated to someone else?

✓ Try to batch your activities so you aren't jumping all over the place all day long. Set up certain times in the day to work on certain types of activities.

✓ Try to block off time each day to get your veggies done.

✓ Try to begin working on your first veggie as quickly as you can after you get to work.

✓ Before you begin working on a task or project, ask yourself, "Is this the best use of my time right now?" Be sure you're working on the right task at the right time.

✓ Organize the night before, not first thing when you get to work.

✓ Be sure to try to get two veggies done every day before lunch.

✓ Have discipline when you get to work. Stop doing so much "relationship building" first thing in the morning.

14

Recognizing and Managing Procrastination

Determine that the thing can and shall be done, and then we shall find the way.

—ABRAHAM LINCOLN

Procrastination is the habit of delaying activities until another day or time. We all procrastinate to some degree and in some form or another. In fact, when I got my first employee review, under the heading of "Procrastination," it said, "Above Average." As someone who used to procrastinate exceptionally well, I'm going to share some strategies I use to keep it in check and under control.

IT'S IMPORTANT TO RECOGNIZE...

1. When we are procrastinating and why
2. What our favorite replacement activities are
3. Steps we can take to manage and overcome our procrastination

MAJOR CAUSES OF PROCRASTINATION

- The task is unpleasant.
- The task is difficult.
- I'm overwhelmed (I have too many tasks to pick from).
- I have too many interruptions back to back.
- I'm not organized, or I lack information.
- I don't have clear or written goals.
- I'm not in the mood.
- I don't see why this task is so important.
- I don't have time now.
- This isn't due for a while.

Activity

Answer the following questions:

1. What things do you put off most often?
2. What things are you currently putting off?
3. How do you know when you are procrastinating?
4. Do you have a favorite set of replacement activities?
5. What activities do you choose instead of doing the task you know you have to complete?

Note: When you put two or more of these together, you're guaranteed to put off that important task or project.

HOW TO MANAGE PROCRASTINATION

The following suggestions, when properly used, can help you "trick" yourself out of procrastinating and into action.

Set Deadlines

If you get tasks or projects without a deadline, be sure to ask for one. Try to get as specific a deadline as possible. If you can't get one, try to give yourself one or make one up. When we have clearly written detailed plan of action, it makes it easier to set priorities and get started. Your mind figures, "If I've put in this much time, I might as well get started." It's all about making the commitment.

Start Every Day with the Most Important Task on Your List

One of the fastest ways to overcome procrastination is to start every day with a task that would make you feel more confident and positive if you could get it out of the way first thing. Often times this will be a task or project you would put off until the afternoon or end of the day. This is the "Veggie Principle" discussed in Module 3. Tackle important tasks when you are at your best, not when you have very little energy left, (the end of the day).

Additionally, could you accomplish more by 12 noon each day which would take the pressure off the afternoon? If a difficult and/or unpleasant task is still on your list when your morning ends, what are the chances you will put it off until tomorrow?

TIPS:

1. Make sure your deadline is realistic and achievable.

2. Start difficult or unpleasant tasks during your most productive time. You'll finish them more quickly.

Do It Once

Have you ever noticed how many piles of papers are on your desk
or how many e-mails are in your in-box? When you first receive a
piece of paper, make a note on the top of it of where it belongs, or
put the task required on your Master List and file it. When you get
an e-mail, take action on it, file it, or delete it. Don't let your work
pile up, and stop duplicating activities when possible. Many times,
your Timekeeping Journal will show you the activities you often
repeat.

Break Down the Job into Smaller Parts

A human tendency is to start tasks that we perceive take short
amounts of time. The number one way to overcome procrastination
is to break your larger task into smaller ones that take about 20 to 30
minutes to complete. In today's busy workplace, it's much easier to
find 20 or 30 minutes than it is to find an hour or more.

By completing smaller tasks, you'll build confidence to get
the job done. Remember: if the task looks easy and won't take
much time, human nature will cause you to choose that task before
others.

A CASE STUDY

June wanted to paint a room in her house. I asked her, "Could you just paint one wall per night?" She said, "Sure. One wall a night, anyone could do that." I said, "Okay, I'll call you tomorrow and see how you did."

When I called her the next day, she said, "Let me tell you what happened. On the way home from work I stopped by Target and got Cher's new CD. I started playing it and began painting. I finished the first wall and thought to myself, 'Why don't I keep on painting? I haven't heard all of my new CD.' So I started on the next wall."

I said, "Don't tell me!" She said, "Yup, I finished the whole room last night. Why did I make a mountain out of a mole hill?"

TIP: This is how I use "underpromise-overdeliver" to work through procrastination. I say to myself, "I'm only going to work on a task or project for 15 minutes." Next thing I know, no one has interrupted me, so I keep going. Then, I start to get interested and have some success. Finally, I look up at the clock and I've been working on it for two hours. It's better to start small than to never start at all.

Cut Down on Interruptions

Interruptions derail us from getting things done. "I could have gotten it done, but the phone rang every five minutes." We're not talking about worthwhile interruptions. We're talking about limiting unnecessary ones. As mentioned earlier, when we are interrupted, it can often take hours, or even days, to come back to what we were working on. When I get interrupted four to five times in a row, I lose focus, and my mind says, "You need a break." That's why I really try to block out time each day to get my veggies done.

TIP: By reducing interruptions, we can concentrate better and finish the task much sooner. Defer the interruption by negotiating a better time for the activity or letting the call go to voice mail, so you can complete the task you're currently working on.

Let Others Know of Your Deadline

Your friends and/or peers will make you accountable. This will also provide excellent motivation, especially when they keep reminding you about your goal and the date that you said you were going to finish by.

Give Yourself a Pep Talk

Difficult and unpleasant tasks can be tough, not only to start but also to finish. You must believe you can do it. Many times, we'll exaggerate how difficult or unpleasant a task will be before we even start. Try becoming your own cheerleader instead.

Eliminate, one by one, "reasons" why you can't start or get the task done. Talk yourself into just starting the task and trying to do it for 20 to 30 minutes. Focus on the reward. You may be surprised the next time you look up to see that you've been working for an hour!

Get More Information and/or Answers to Your Questions

Pick up the phone or get out of your chair and get the information or answers you need to overcome roadblocks. If it's important, don't wait. Often, the smallest piece of information or the smallest question answered will get us jumpstarted again. Don't use the excuse of not having enough information to put off tasks.

Create a Reward

Before you start that difficult or unpleasant task, think of a way to reward yourself when you complete it. It could be a new outfit, a meal at an expensive restaurant, a much-needed vacation, or just something you really like to do. Put that carrot in front of you so you see what's in it for you to complete that task.

People talk about improving the quality of their personal lives. Why not start by giving yourself mini-rewards that improve the quality of your personal life? Of course, you can always wait and hope until the end of the year!

QUICK TIPS

✓ Try to figure out when you're procrastinating and why.

✓ Identify what you like and don't like to do at work and home.

✓ If a task or project seems too difficult or large, start by brainstorming and look for ways to break it into manageable chunks.

✓ If you can't decide which task or project to start on, ask your leader.

✓ Avoid too many back-to-back interruptions, or you'll become unfocused.

✓ If you don't know how to do a task, ask someone. Don't wait for osmosis.

✓ Try to see the end result of the project in your mind, and work backward.

✓ If you're not interested in a task or project, see if you can switch with someone else.

✓ Don't block out large chunks of time to work on tasks or projects, or you may never start.

✓ Even if a project isn't due for a while, start working on it immediately so you don't have to do it all at the end.

✓ If you didn't get a start date from your leader, ask for one.

✓ Block off time to work on important projects so you can cut down on interruptions.

✓ If you sit in a high-traffic area and you need to concentrate on something, go work somewhere else like a conference room.

✓ Let others know of your deadline so they'll leave you alone.

✓ Give yourself a pep talk.

✓ Create a reward for finishing tasks you normally put off. (The reward should be equal to the difficulty of the task or project.)

APPENDIX

Time Management Action Plan

Name three time management strategies, discussed in the book, that you're going to implement as soon as you go back to work:

1. _____

2. _____

3. _____

Name one strategy in each of the following areas that you're going to implement within the next seven days:

1. Taking control of your day

_____

2. Project management

_____

3. Organizing

_____

4. Managing priorities

_____

5. Finding more time

_____

6. Controlling your desk

_____

7. Handling interruptions

_____

8. Managing, controlling, and writing e-mail

_____

9. Managing the phone and using voice mail

_____

10. Delegating

_____

11. Planning meetings

_____

12. Managing procrastination

_____

Index

About the Author

Kenneth Zeigler is a top expert on leadership, time management, organization, and productivity improvement. He has authored many articles on these subjects, and he was the first author to discover the problem is not the system people use, but rather their organization skill set.

Ken has served in senior management at firms such as Pillsbury, Hughes, Quaker Oats, Merrill Lynch, and Dean Witter. As a consultant he has advised clients such as the Federal Reserve, the U.S. Treasury, the Bureau of Veterans Affairs, ING, PNC Bank, PPG, MetLife, Hormel, Hertz, Cooper Tire & Rubber, and California law enforcement.

Ken attended the University of Minnesota as an undergraduate, where he was a member of the varsity football team, and then completed graduate work in advertising and finance at the University of Illinois. He lives in Charlotte with his wife Mary Beth and his sons, Zachary and Nicholas.

Visit his Web site at http://www.kztraining.com. As you read this book you may have specific questions on how to apply the tips, tools, ideas, and strategies discussed in this book. Please e-mail your questions to Ken Zeigler at kzeigler2@gmail.com and he will respond directly to you.